30 DAY EUCHARISTIC REVIVAL

A Retreat with St. Peter Julian Eymard

DONALD H. CALLOWAY, MIC

with Patrick O'Hearn

Available from:
Marian Helpers Center, Stockbridge, MA 01263

Prayerline: 1-800-804-3823
Orderline: 1-800-462-7426

Websites:
FatherCalloway.org
Marian.org

Publication Date: January 1, 2024
Solemnity of Mary, Mother of God

Library of Congress Control Number: 2023944721
ISBN: 978-1-59614-601-3

Imprimi Potest:
Very Rev. Chris Alar, MIC, Provincial Superior
The Blessed Virgin Mary, Mother of Mercy Province
August 2, 2023
Feast of St. Peter Julian Eymard

Nihil Obstat:
Robert A. Stackpole, STD, Censor Deputatus
August 2, 2023

Note: The *Nihil Obstat* and corresponding *Imprimi Potest* are not a certification that those granting it agree with the contents, opinions, or statements expressed in the work. Instead, they merely confirm that the work contains nothing contrary to faith and morals.

Cover image by Christopher Santer

Special thanks to Mr. & Mrs. Patrick and Amanda O'Hearn, Mr. & Mrs. Steven and Maureen O'Hearn, Mr. & Mrs. Donald and LaChita Calloway, Matthew Calloway, Ileana E. Salazar, Teresa de Jesus Macias, Milanka Lachman, Tad Floridis, Bethany Price, Mrs. Valerie Lemariey, and the Curia Generalizia of the Congregation of the Blessed Sacrament.

To
Our Lady of the Blessed Sacrament
and
St. Joseph, Guardian of the Heavenly Manna

Table of Contents

Amen, amen, I say to you, unless you eat the flesh of the Son of man and drink his blood, you have no life in you. Whoever eats my flesh and drinks my blood has eternal life, and I will raise him up at the last day. For my flesh is food indeed, and my blood is true drink.

— John 6:53–55

A retreat is the greatest of all graces because it contains all the graces of conversion and of spiritual renovation in the Christian life. When God wants to convert a soul, he gives it the grace of a retreat. We all have need of conversion; for we have defects and carry the "old man" in us.

— St. Peter Julian Eymard

Introduction

I have often reflected upon the remedies for the universal indifference which is taking hold of so many Catholics in a frightening way. I can find only one: the Eucharist, love for Jesus Eucharistic. Loss of faith comes in the first place from loss of love; darkness, from the loss of light; the freezing cold of death from the absence of fire.[1]

— St. Peter Julian Eymard

In *Consecration to St. Joseph: The Wonders of Our Spiritual Father*, St. Peter Julian Eymard is the first saint I reference. His wisdom and insights on St. Joseph are tremendous and almost without parallel. More importantly, St. Peter Julian Eymard loved the Holy Eucharist. His zeal for preaching on the Eucharist and promoting Eucharistic adoration is the reason several popes have referred to St. Peter Julian Eymard as "the Apostle of the Eucharist."

Nonetheless, St. Peter Julian Eymard is not that well known in the universal Church. France and several other countries in Europe promote his works, but when it comes to worldwide recognition of his extraordinary life, as well as the many amazing things he did to foster a greater love for the Blessed Sacrament, most Catholics are unfamiliar with him and have never heard his name. That is about to change.

In early 2022, Patrick O'Hearn, a Catholic author (www.patrickrohearn.com) and lover of the saints, contacted me and shared an idea that was on his heart. He had noted how often I referenced the "Apostle of the Eucharist" in *Consecration to St. Joseph* and figured I had a devotion to him. He suggested that I write a retreat-style book on the Holy Eucharist based on the wisdom and insights of St. Peter Julian Eymard. I loved the idea and asked him for further thoughts and assistance in giving the project direction. With great zeal for wanting to make St. Peter Julian Eymard better known, Patrick scoured through the writings of St. Peter Julian Eymard, gathering quotes on the Eucharist, and sent me a rudimentary thematic outline that could serve for a possible book. It was a great start for the book. The work Patrick did was invaluable, and I am forever grateful to him for his brotherhood and incredible idea.

But there was a bump in the road.

As the book neared completion, I was informed that the Congregation of the Blessed Sacrament — a religious community founded by St. Peter Julian Eymard — was in the process of gathering, authenticating, translating, and publishing the critical edition of the writings of St. Peter Julian Eymard.[2] I was overjoyed with the news but then learned that the critical edition of St. Peter Julian Eymard's writings were only available in French, not English. To date, it remains uncertain when the critical English edition will be finished.[3] This left me with a dilemma. Should I wait until the critical English edition of his works is available before publishing *30 Day Eucharistic Revival?* It would mean delaying the book, possibly for several years. With the manuscript for *30 Day Eucharistic Revival* complete and a publication date set, what was I to do?

Pray.

Prayer was the most important thing to be done.

With prayer, as well as consultation with the Congregation of the Blessed Sacrament in the United States and Rome, I decided not to wait to publish *30 Day Eucharistic Revival.* There is an urgency to the book. It can't wait! "What's the rush?" you might ask. Well, Catholics in the United States are currently undergoing a severe crisis of belief in the Real Presence of Jesus in the Blessed Sacrament. We need to do something about it now!

Let me explain.

Several years ago, a survey in the United States revealed that 69 percent of Catholics no longer believe in the Real Presence of Jesus in the Blessed Sacrament (Holy Communion).

Looking at it from another perspective, this means that only 31 percent of Catholics in the United States believe in the *source and summit* of the Christian faith. This is a tragedy!

In response to this crisis, the United States Conference of Catholic Bishops (USCCB) initiated a "Eucharistic Revival." It involves several years of teaching, preaching, and events that are intended to help turn things around. The Eucharistic Revival concludes on Pentecost Sunday in 2025. It's a noble initiative and one that I pray bears good fruit. Returning to belief in the Real Presence is an urgent matter and of the utmost importance in the life of the Church. My desire is to offer the Church a book on the Eucharist grounded in the wisdom and insights of the Apostle of the Eucharist. Publishing such a book is an urgent matter. I think St. Peter Julian Eymard would agree because he dealt with similar crises of belief in the Real Presence in his time.

Saint Peter Julian Eymard lived in an era that was plagued by lack of belief in the Real Presence and outright indifference to this core teaching of Christianity. His response was to act quickly. He wrote,

> Now we must quickly get to work to save souls by the divine Eucharist, to awaken France and Europe numbed in dormant apathy because they don't know the gift of God, Jesus, the Eucharistic Emmanuel. This is the torch of love which we must carry to tepid souls who think they are devout, and are not, because they haven't made Jesus in the holy tabernacle their center and their life. Any devotion which doesn't set up one tent on Calvary, and one near the tabernacle, is not a solid piety and will never do anything great. I fear that people are wandering too far from the Holy Eucharist, that this mystery of love par excellence is not sufficiently proclaimed. So souls are suffering, becoming more sensual and materialistic in their devotional life

and inordinately attached to human beings. It is because they don't know how to find their consolation and strength in our Lord.[4]

I feel the same urgency today as St. Peter Julian Eymard did in his day. God's people need a greater love for the Eucharist. If people center their lives on the Eucharist, it will prove to be a remedy for the problems of our time.

For this reason, I want to do something that will bless the Church in these current crises and for all future generations. The Eucharistic Revival of the USCCB will come and go, but a book that offers God's people wisdom on the Eucharist from the Apostle of the Eucharist will be timeless. Sprinkle in other saints and what they said about the Eucharist, and it will be a book to be used for generations to come. *30 Day Eucharistic Revival* is intended to help you, your children, your grandchildren, and all future generations rediscover and experience a revival of belief in the Real Presence. May the Eucharistic Revival never end!

— Fr. Donald H. Calloway, MIC

Meet the Retreat Master:
St. Peter Julian Eymard

Before you begin *30 Day Eucharistic Revival*, allow me to introduce the Retreat Master, St. Peter Julian Eymard. He was born on February 4, 1811, in La Mure d'Isere, France, a small town in the southeastern region of the country. From his infancy, St. Peter's mother instilled a love for the Eucharist in her son. Often, she carried her infant son to Benediction so that he could experience the Real Presence of Jesus in the Blessed Sacrament. Later, as a young boy, he would frequently accompany his mother on her daily visit to the Blessed Sacrament. On one occasion, his sister found her five-year-old brother next to the tabernacle with his ear pressed against it while standing on a stepladder. When she asked him why he was so close to the tabernacle, the burgeoning apostle of the Eucharist said he wanted to hear Jesus.

From an early age, Peter wanted to be a priest. However, as the only surviving son of his parents, his father opposed his vocation. This was especially true after his mother passed away. He once commented, "In my mother's death, my father found a new weapon against my vocation."[1] Yet God's will could not be stopped. Following his father's death, he was able to fulfill his call. He studied and was ordained a priest for the Diocese of Grenoble on July 20, 1834. He was 23 years old when he became a priest.

Throughout his priestly ministry, he expressed a great love for the Virgin Mary and St. Joseph and loved to preach Eucharistic devotions. He was a personal friend of St. John Vianney, and was known to frequently visit the apparition site of Our Lady of La Salette where Mary appeared in 1846. This site was about 94 miles from his hometown.

One day, as he was carrying the Blessed Sacrament in a procession at St. Paul's Church in Lyon, he had a moving experience that convicted him to devote his entire priestly life to promoting the truth of the Real Presence. Up to this point, his focus when preaching on the Eucharist had been one of reparation, because the heresy of Jansenism was running rampant in France and many other parts of Europe. Jansenism's main theme is mankind's unworthiness and sinfulness in relation to God. But during the Eucharistic procession in Lyon, he realized that even though reparation to the Blessed Sacrament was needed, the real emphasis of devotion to the Eucharist should be love: Jesus' love for us, and our love for him. After this experience, St. Peter's great mission as a priest was initiated: to ignite the hearts of the faithful with a burning love of the Holy Eucharist!

His zeal for the Eucharist led him to found two religious communities dedicated to promoting adoration of the Blessed Sacrament: the Congregation of the Blessed Sacrament for men, and the Servants of the Blessed Sacrament for women. He also promoted 40 Hours Eucharistic Adoration, nocturnal adoration, and perpetual adoration. For the rest of his life, he never tired of preaching and writing about the Blessed Sacrament. Although he has not been declared a Doctor of the Church, he deserves the honor and would be a worthy candidate for being declared the "Doctor of the Eucharist." His writings on the Eucharist are akin to a doctor giving prescriptions to his patients. In his writings we find a cure for every vice, for his remedy is always the same: devoutly receive and adore the Holy Eucharist.

Having spent his priesthood fostering love for the Holy Eucharist, St. Peter Julian Eymard died on August 1, 1869, at the age of 57. First buried in the cemetery next to his home parish in La Mure, his tomb was opened in 1877 so that his body could be transferred to Paris. At the time, his body was found to be incorrupt. Today, only his bones remain in the Corpus Christi Chapel in Paris. He was beatified on July 12, 1925, by Pope Pius XI and canonized on December 9, 1962, by Pope St. John XXIII. His feast day is August 2.

Saint Peter Julian Eymard's incredible life and mission have remained hidden in the life of the Church. He once stated the following about himself: "God gives me the grace to suffer everything with joy for the establishment of his Eucharistic kingdom, to esteem as the greatest grace to be unnoticed and unknown by society and by religious people."[2] Now, the time has come to make him known.

— **Patrick O'Hearn**

Retreat Preparation

Many people often lament that they do not have the time to make a retreat or enter into deep thought, prayer, and reflection on the Blessed Sacrament. *30 Day Eucharistic Revival* is an answer to that prayer. Our Retreat Master notes,

> You should have a book on the Blessed Sacrament, that you read a bit every day; do not fear exhausting the matter; the depths of the love of Jesus cannot be measured. Jesus in the Eucharist is the same as in heaven: he is beautiful, ever new, and always infinite. We cannot exhaust him.[1]

30 Day Eucharistic Revival can be done before the Blessed Sacrament, in your home, or wherever you are on any given day. It is up to you to determine how much time you spend reading, meditating, praying, and reflecting on the daily readings. The retreat can also be done any time of the year, and you can begin on any day you like. You can do it individually or with others.

Each of the 30 days consists of the following:

1. Eucharistic wisdom (in blue) from the Retreat Master, St. Peter Julian Eymard
2. Reflections from the author (Fr. Calloway) pertaining to the theme of the day
3. Reflection Questions
4. Resolution
5. Prayer
6. Litany of the Holy Eucharist / Litany of the Most Precious Blood (*alternating days*)

As you read, ponder, and meditate on the readings, if a word or phrase from St. Peter Julian Eymard's writings grabs your attention, take time to ponder it more deeply. The retreat is designed to facilitate conversation with our Eucharistic Lord and help you fall more in love with the Blessed Sacrament.

Know how to tell the Good God what you think, what you desire, what you grieve over. Talk simply and artlessly with our Lord as if you held conversation with your own soul. Be a child full of love and openheartedness toward this good Master. And in this labor of love do not speak all the time, but know how to remain silent at the feet of Jesus; find your joy in seeing him, in contemplating him, in listening to him, and in realizing that you are in his presence; the real language of love is rather interior than exterior.[2]

— St. Peter Julian Eymard

THE RETREAT

DAY 1
God's Eternal Love

Retreat Master: St. Peter Julian Eymard

There is a truth on which we must meditate all our lives and it is this: God has loved us from all eternity. We have always existed in the good God's love, we have always been present in the thoughts of the Holy Trinity: the Father thought of his creature, the Son of those whom he would redeem, the Holy Spirit of those whom he would sanctify.

God has always loved me! Wonderful thought which shows our greatness and the nobility of our origin. Even before our actual existence, we already lived in a certain sense in God: He saw us, he loved us with a well-wishing love, as a mother already loves her child which she carries in her womb. He pressed us to his heart: "This is that little creature which will be born at a certain time, in certain circumstances, who will have a certain grace, and who will love me!" That truth should produce gratitude in us.

The good God loves us with a benevolent love: He does not love us for profit, for he does not need us. He has loved us therefore solely to convey love to us, an absolute gratuitous love: He loves us in order to make us happy. He gives us everything without any selfishness, for we can do nothing to augment his glory and his happiness.[1]

Reflection

God loves you!

He has loved you from all eternity.

He loves us in order to make us happy.

The love of God is the foundation of creation and Christianity. Our finite minds find it hard to wrap themselves around the reality that we have been loved into existence and mean so much to God, so much that he became man in order to suffer and save us from sin. Yet it is true. God loves us. God loves you! He did not have to create us or save us. He is not under any obligation or necessity to bring us into existence or rescue us from darkness. But he did.

God acts as if he cannot live without us, even dying for us and choosing to remain with us in what appears to be an insignificant piece of bread. Can there be any greater self-giving, self-emptying love than this? God is so in love with us that he seems to be mad! It's such a radical kind of love that God has for us that St. Catherine of Siena and St. Faustina Kowalska considered God to be a divine madman because of his "crazy" love for sinful creatures.

If you accept — and you should — the Christian truth that God loves you, and that he wants to be with you and have you with him in paradise, everything in your life changes. Everything in your life will reflect that reality. Knowing that God is "madly" in love with you gives you the ability to endure all things and overcome all things. God's love puts things into an eternal perspective. Come calamity, hardship, heartbreak, disease, and even death, you are grounded and unshakable. You know that God is always with you and has you in mind. He can't stop thinking about you.

In this Eucharistic retreat, God wants to affirm you in his love. He wants to give you the absolute certainty that you are loved. No matter what your perception of God has been before this retreat, open your heart to the fundamental Christian truth that "God is love" (1 John 4:8). Not only that, he wants you to know that his love is most perfectly revealed and available to you in the Eucharist. There is no greater love possible. This side of eternity, the Holy Eucharist is the closest you will get to God. The Blessed Sacrament is the extension of the Incarnation; God is so in love with you that he took on flesh and blood in order to be physically near you, and continues to be near you every single day of your life in the Blessed Sacrament. Love doesn't get more real, intimate, and intense than in Holy Communion.

Over the next 30 days, surrender yourself to God's love. Ponder and meditate on the wisdom of St. Peter Julian Eymard, the Apostle of the Eucharist. Through the wisdom and insights of our Retreat Master, Jesus wants you to know that you are loved. Jesus wants you to know that he wants to share the greatest of his treasures with you and be consumed by you!

Reflection Questions

1. Why is God's eternal love the foundation of Christianity?
2. Do you truly believe that God loves you?
3. How does the reality of God's love change everything in your life?

Resolution

Today, rest in the knowledge of God's eternal love for you. Be still and know that he knows your name, everything about you, and has always loved you. He's looking at you right now.

Prayer

Dear Jesus, my Eucharistic Lord, thank you for your eternal love. I want to love you with all my being. Grant me every grace I need this day to reciprocate your love. I want to be close to you. On this retreat, open my heart to a fresh and true understanding of your love for me. Give me a new relationship and a newfound love for the Blessed Sacrament. Our Lady of the Blessed Sacrament, untie any of the knots and lies that cause me to doubt God's love for me. Saint Joseph, my spiritual father, be with me on this retreat and bring about a Eucharistic revival in my soul. Saint Peter Julian Eymard, Apostle of the Eucharist, fill me with your Eucharistic zeal so that I might love the Blessed Sacrament above all things.

Pray the Litany of the Holy Eucharist (page 163)

DAY 2
God's Personal Love

Retreat Master: St. Peter Julian Eymard

What makes God's love so much stronger and more powerful is that it is personal, given particularly to every one of us as if there is no one else in all the world.

God loves you personally; for you alone he created the world and all its wonders; for love of you alone he became man and desired to be your guide, your servant, your friend, your defender, and your companion in the journey from time to eternity.

For you alone he instituted the Sacrament of Baptism, in which you became, through the grace and merits of Jesus Christ, the child of God and heir of the eternal kingdom; for you alone he sends the Holy Spirit, his person and his gifts.

In the Eucharist, you receive for yourself alone the person of the Son of God, the two natures of Jesus Christ, his glories and his graces; for your own sins you have an all-powerful victim of propitiation, perpetually immolated.

In the Sacrament of Penance, God has prepared for you an efficacious remedy for all your maladies, a balm that even raises from the dead.

To sanctify you, he has established his priesthood, proceeding from himself in an uninterrupted succession.

For you, he has supernaturalized and sanctified the marriage bond and has made it the symbol of his union with the Church.

For you, he has prepared a holy Viaticum full of sweetness and strength to aid you in your supreme hour. He has placed at your side his angels and his saints, his august mother herself, to keep you, help you, console you, and support you.

For you, he has prepared a magnificent throne in heaven where he intends to load you with honor and glory, where you shall enjoy the blissful vision of the Most Holy Trinity, contemplated and comprehended directly, without veil or intermediary.

Once having understood these divine truths, you should be unable to contain your love; you should live for love and be consumed by love.[1]

Reflection

For you, God has done everything.

He loves you personally.

Live for love! Be consumed by love!

Jesus will never abandon you, disappoint you, or hurt you. He is good, and his Heavenly Father is the best of fathers.

Isn't all of the above a comforting thought? You are loved by the Almighty, the Alpha and the Omega, the God who is Father God. Perhaps you have never known the kind and generous love of a father. But that doesn't change who God is or alter his paternal love for you. He wants you to know that his love is so personal, his loving concern for you so paternal, that he had you in mind for all eternity. He loves you so much that he planned for your well-being long before you even came into existence. He has prepared for you Baptism, Confirmation, Confession, the Holy Eucharist, the Sacrament of Matrimony or the Sacrament of Holy Orders, and Anointing of the Sick. You lack nothing because of God's personal love. Even those called to religious life, consecrated virginity, or who have a special mission in the Church of remaining single for the glory of God and the kingdom of heaven have had everything prepared in advance. Your loving Father has given the Church all the graces and blessings you will need during your entire life. You are loved personally. You are not forgotten.

Sometimes people think that God has forgotten them or doesn't love them. Do you think this way? Without a doubt, we all have different backgrounds, experiences, and stories that make us who we are. Perhaps your journey has been a rough one, filled with twists and turns, setbacks, failures, heartbreak, and pain. This is true for many people. But God is not overcome by your struggles in life. Not at all. He can handle you and all your complexities, weaknesses, and problems. Your problems are not problems for God. They are opportunities for him to shower his love on you. Remember: the squeaky wheel gets the grease; the child with the most wounds receives the most kisses.

Even though there are billions of people on the planet, God has you in mind and loves you personally. Numbers are nothing to God. The cosmos and all of its vastness and expanse are as a speck of dust to God. You are what he loves most. You.

When you come to understand the profound love that God has for you and that the greatest expression of his love for you is in the Blessed Sacrament, you will come to understand just how much he loves you personally. Don't you want to know that? Don't you want to experience such love from the all-powerful God that it appears as if you are the only object of his love? Well, you can. The Eucharist is the divine fire of God's personal love for you. You will never find a greater love anywhere else.

Nothing in life will ever fully satisfy you like the Blessed Sacrament. As wonderful as pristine beaches, mountain getaways, majestic sunsets, treasured friendships, adorable babies, and marital bliss are, nothing compares to God's personal love in Holy Communion. This doesn't mean that all the other things are not wonderful gifts from God. They are. Yet, as wonderful as they are, they are all temporal and finite. In Holy Communion, God is offering you something greater. He is giving you himself.

Reflection Questions

1. Do you believe that God loves you personally?
2. Why is the Holy Eucharist the greatest expression of God's personal love for you?
3. How does God's personal love change your life, thoughts, and actions?

Resolution

Today, rest in God's personal love for you. He is still looking at you. He doesn't change. He is the same yesterday, today, and forever. Ask for a Eucharistic revival in your soul.

Prayer

Dear Jesus, my Eucharistic Lord, thank you for your personal love for me. You thought of everything I would need to make me happy and holy when you created me. My life is in your hands, and I want to enter into a deeper and greater love for you than I have ever had before. I want to love you personally because I know that you love me personally. Our Lady of the Most Blessed Sacrament, thank you for loving me as your child and for desiring me to experience a Eucharistic revival. Saint Joseph, help me to live for love and be consumed by love. Saint Peter Julian Eymard, Apostle of the Eucharist, fill me with your Eucharistic zeal so that I might love the Blessed Sacrament above all things.

Pray the Litany of the Most Precious Blood (page 166)

DAY 3
Jesus' Eucharistic Love

Retreat Master: St. Peter Julian Eymard

What end did Jesus Christ have in mind in instituting the Divine Eucharist? He wanted man to love him above all things. Yes, Jesus Christ instituted the Most Blessed Sacrament of the Altar in order to be loved by man, to possess his heart, to be the principle of his life.[1]

Without the Eucharist, Christ's love would be nothing more for us than a lifeless love, a love of the past, which we would quickly forget and which it would be almost excusable for us to forget. Love has its laws, its requirements, which the Eucharist alone satisfies. On account of the Eucharist Jesus has every right to be loved because in it he gives us a proof of infinite love.[2]

In his Passion, he spared not his divine life; nor does he spare it in the Eucharist. His glory, majesty, and power are not seen in the Host. He is only the Man of Sorrows.

Jesus in his Passion allowed only his love to appear. Woe to them who will not recognize it! Only a thief, a robber, adored his Divinity and proclaimed his innocence; only nature deplored its Creator.

In the Blessed Sacrament, Jesus with still more love continues this immolation of his attributes. Of all the power of Jesus Christ, of all his glory, we behold only patience so great that it would almost scandalize if we did not know that his love for us is infinite, that it is even foolishness!

Our sweet Savior seems to say to us: "Have I not done enough for you? Do I not deserve your love? What can I do more? Try to think of some sacrifice that I may still make!"

> The Eucharist is the supreme proof of Jesus' love for us, because it is the supreme sacrifice.[3]

Reflection

Jesus instituted the Eucharist in order to be loved by you.
He wants to possess your heart.
He wants to be the principle of your life.
Everyone knows that love makes a person do "crazy" things. Love is universal, and we have all done crazy things for love. God did, too. He emptied himself completely for his beloved. You are his beloved. What more could he give than to create a way to be consumed by you and live in you? Divine love does crazy things.

Have you ever picked up a cute little baby and smothered it with kisses, making unintelligible, nonsensical noises as you pretend to eat the baby, nibbling on the infant's chubby little belly? Sure you have. We all have. Did you perhaps also say to the child as you tickled him, "I'm gonna eat you up! Yes, I am! Yes, I am!" You probably have. We all have enough common sense, however, to know that such expressions of loving affection are "crazy" and not meant to be taken literally. In other words, we don't eat babies. Nobody in their right mind would do that. That's bad. Really bad. But this "crazy" expression of love does convey something amazing about how much God loves us and wants to be consumed by us.

Thousands of years ago a baby was born. That baby is a divine person. He came into the world to be adored and give his flesh to eat. His flesh gives eternal life. He is Jesus, the Son of God and the Son of Mary. He is your God and the lover of your soul. He is so crazy in love with you that he contrived a way to be so intimately united with you that when you consume him you have eternal life. He is true food. It's in the Bible.

Amen, amen, I say to you, unless you eat the flesh of the Son of man and drink his blood, you have no life in you. Whoever eats my flesh and drinks my blood has eternal life, and I will raise him up at the last day. For my flesh is food indeed, and my blood is true drink. (John 6:53–55)

Pretty shocking stuff, right? But he meant it. The Eucharist is not a symbol, a sign, or only a wafer on a tray. No. The Eucharist is an extension of the Incarnation of Jesus Christ. The Eucharist is Jesus Christ. We are talking about a divine person who took on flesh, became an adorable little baby, grew into the fullness of his manhood, and invented a way to be consumed by you. He did all this because he wanted to leave to his Church the food that gives everlasting life. He gave the Church the Eucharist for you!

To love is to wish to be perpetually present to the person loved: that is the Blessed Eucharist, the Real Presence. To love is to give oneself to each of those whom one loves: that is Holy Communion.[4]
— Venerable Louise Margaret Claret de la Touche

Throughout the centuries, non-Catholics have sometimes thought that because Catholics believe the Eucharist is the literal Body and Blood of Jesus that Catholics practice a form of cannibalism. What they don't understand is that the Body and Blood of Jesus in Holy Communion, while truly his Body and Blood, is offered to us in an unbloody manner. The Eucharist is the everlasting memorial and re-presentation of the sacrifice of Jesus on the Cross. Yet it's more than just a memory of Jesus. The Eucharist is Jesus. He is the Lamb of God who takes away our sins. As the Israelites in the Old Testament consumed the sacrificial lamb at Passover, Catholics consume the Lamb of God (Jesus in the Blessed Sacrament) through sacramental reception. The Body and Blood we receive in Holy Communion is the same Body and Blood that was present in Mary's womb, in the manger at Bethlehem, in the home of Nazareth, in the Upper Room, on the Cross, in heaven, and at every Holy Sacrifice of the Mass. It isn't cannibalism. It's divine, crazy love finding a way to be consumed! God loves you so much that he didn't want you to wait until heaven to be united with him. He knows that the journey to paradise is filled with suffering, difficulty, and hardship. He has provided the food that will get you there. He is the way, the truth, and the life. There is no other way to the Father than through Jesus Christ.

Do you believe this? Do you understand this? It's an essential teaching of Christianity. It's what makes Christianity different from all other religions. Jesus is God, not a guru or a wise teacher. He is your food. He became a baby for you. He continues to become bread for you. He loves you so much that he was murdered for you and is now with you always in the Blessed Sacrament. Christianity is not a philosophy or an idea; it's a relationship with the God of love — the God who *is* love.

If someone asked you to provide a reason for your belief in the Real Presence of Jesus in the Eucharist, what would you say? Our Retreat Master has the perfect response: "Many answers could be given to that question. The one that sums them all runs as follows: because he loves us and because he wants us to love him. Love, that is the motive for the institution of the Eucharist."[5]

The Eucharist is above all a sacrament of love.[6]

— Blessed Michael Sopoćko

If you want to make the Blessed Sacrament the principle of your life, our Retreat Master offers the following advice:

And now, how will you respond to the love of a God who wants to be loved uniquely by you, who wants to be the sole end of your life, of your mind, and of your heart? Let us ask his pardon for having passed so much of our life without loving him; let us thank him, let us live on gratitude, and thus we shall return to him the fruits of the grace of which we robbed him in loving him too little up to this day.[7]

Reflection Questions

1. Why did our Lord choose the Holy Eucharist to show us his love?
2. What keeps you from loving our Eucharistic Lord above all things?
3. How can you make the Holy Eucharist the principle of your life?

Resolution

Today, ask our Eucharistic Lord to take possession of your heart and your life. Invite him to be the principle of your life. Let him know that you are grateful that he came to save you and be consumed by you in Holy Communion.

Prayer

Dear Jesus, my Eucharistic Lord, thank you for the Holy Eucharist, the greatest proof of your ongoing love for me. Grant me every grace I need this day to become who you created me to be. Forgive me for the times I have taken for granted or offended your Real Presence in the Blessed Sacrament. Our Lady of the Most Blessed Sacrament, place in my heart an insatiable desire to consume the saving flesh of your divine infant, the God-man Jesus Christ. Saint Joseph, set my heart aflame with love for Holy Communion! Saint Peter Julian Eymard, Apostle of the Eucharist, fill me with your Eucharistic zeal so that I might love the Blessed Sacrament above all things.

Pray the Litany of the Holy Eucharist (page 163)

DAY 4
Love Is Not Loved

Retreat Master: St. Peter Julian Eymard

Alas! It is but too true: our Lord in the most Blessed Sacrament is not loved! He is not loved by the millions of pagans and infidels, by the millions of schismatics and heretics who either know nothing of the Eucharist or have wrong notions of it.[1]

Even among Catholics, few, very few love Jesus in the Most Blessed Sacrament. How many think of him frequently, speak of him, come to adore him and receive him? What is the reason for this forgetfulness and coldness? Oh! They have never tasted the Eucharist, its sweetness, the delights of its love![2]

Reflection

Love is not loved.

Even many Catholics do not love Jesus in the Most Blessed Sacrament.

You can do something about it!

Why is Jesus loved so little in the Blessed Sacrament? There are many reasons — too many to list here — but bad catechesis, rampant liturgical abuses, and the workings of the devil are a few reasons. What is very sad, as our Retreat Master notes and recent surveys prove, is that even many Catholics do not properly love Jesus in the Blessed Sacrament. Many Catholics live as though Jesus is not present in Holy Communion. As a result, many Catholics do not receive him worthily, never visit him, adore him, or speak of his Real Presence to others.

Our Retreat Master believed that one of the root causes for indifference and lack of belief in the Real Presence is that "we ignore or do not sufficiently look into the sacrifices made by his love for our sake."[3] Our Retreat Master goes on to note that "it cost our Savior the whole Passion to institute the Eucharist."⁴ Have you ever considered these aspects of the Eucharist that our Retreat Master mentions? Have you ever thought about the tremendous love and sacrifice it required of Jesus to institute and give you the Eucharist?

The Eucharist was instituted by Jesus because he loves you and sacrificed himself for you, undergoing tremendous suffering, even being stripped naked, beaten, and murdered in front of his mother. He was abandoned, dragged through the streets of Jerusalem, forced to carry a cross, scourged, crowned with thorns, spit on, mocked, humiliated, and crucified to show us his love and bequeath to us his Body and Blood in Holy Communion. There is no greater love.

Think about it: If a person treated his friends the way so many Catholics treat the Holy Eucharist, they would soon find themselves having no friends. Yet how many Catholics receive Holy Communion in a haphazard way? How many commit sacrilege by receiving Holy Communion in mortal sin? How many priests and bishops allow liturgical abuses, idols and false gods to be set up in sanctuaries, immodest attire in church, and tabernacles to be placed in closets or locations where nobody can find him? Has Jesus done something wrong that his Real Presence in the tabernacle is so often banished to corridors and corners of the church? Why has he been hidden behind a wall, out of view of the entire congregation? It's horrible what has taken place in recent years. Love is not loved.

> How shall we repay our loving Redeemer for so much love? We must render love for love. In return for the gift of his Sacred Heart we must give him our hearts without reserve. To return our Lord love for love, we must offer our love wholly and completely to him. He has given us his heart for all eternity; we must give him ours forever.⁵
>
> — St. John Eudes

Hidden Jesus, Eternal Love, our Source of Life, Divine Madman, in that you forget yourself and see only us. Before creating heaven and earth, you carried us in the depths of your heart. O Love, O depth of your abasement, O mystery of happiness, why do so few people know you? Why is your love not returned?[6]

— St. Faustina Kowalska

Are you willing to love Jesus in the Eucharist and give him your heart? Might you return love for love and receive Holy Communion reverently, visit the Blessed Sacrament occasionally, and make it a point never to receive him in mortal sin?

If you are a priest or a bishop, you have the ability to make correctives in your parish or diocese so that love is loved. A Eucharistic revival that does not proclaim a return to reverence, as well as placing tabernacles back in the sanctuary, will bear little lasting fruit. Don't be afraid, brothers. Be a hero. Do it for Jesus! Do it for souls!

I do not want in my life as a bishop, like before in my life as a priest, that my soul be distressed except for one single disgrace, which is the biggest of all: the abandonment of the tabernacle. And that it may rejoice in only one sole happiness: the tabernacle accompanied.[7]

— St. Manuel González García

Reflection Questions

1. Why is the Holy Eucharist loved so little by the world, especially many Catholics?
2. Do you believe you are sufficiently loving our Eucharistic Lord?
3. When is the last time you spoke of the Blessed Sacrament to others? Have you ever done it?

Resolution

Today, resolve to love our Eucharistic Lord more than ever before. Think of the Blessed Sacrament throughout your day and tell Jesus that you love him and long to be before the tabernacle and receive him in Holy Communion. Offer him your love.

Prayer

Dear Jesus, my Eucharistic Lord, have mercy on me for loving you so little. I give you my heart in exchange for your Sacred Heart and desire to more worthily honor your Real Presence. I give you all my love. Our Lady of the Most Blessed Sacrament, help me to love Jesus in the Holy Eucharist and think of him often throughout the day. Saint Joseph, inflame my heart with gratitude and love for our Eucharistic King. Saint Peter Julian Eymard, Apostle of the Eucharist, fill me with your Eucharistic zeal so that I might love the Blessed Sacrament above all things.

Pray the Litany of the Most Precious Blood (page 166)

DAY 5
Sin

Retreat Master: St. Peter Julian Eymard

A retreat purifies the soul from sin, above all, from the habit of sin and affection to sin.[1]

What displeases God most on earth and in us is sin. You must give this truth your attentive consideration. The just and the saints themselves are not exempt from sin. And we, have we not at least venial sins on our conscience? Have we never had to weep for mortal sins?

There is only one evil on earth, only one thing which should fill us with dread: sin. All created things please God, even those which seem obnoxious to us: neither the earthworm nor mud are offensive in the sight of God. Those things are in their natural state. Sin, on the contrary, is a perversion of the divine will, a degradation of God's work, a contradiction to his nature and to his divine being. Sin is an offense and an insult to God's sovereign authority, to his majesty, and to his empire; it is an insult of the creature to its Creator.[2]

How good God has been not to strike me down at once after my sin! And yet I deserve it. If he had condemned me, I would have had nothing to say. Therefore, how good God is not to have abandoned me!

We are not sufficiently afraid of sin, and when we have committed it, we have not enough courage to atone for it as we should. We are full of hope, and say to ourselves, "I will confess when I fall ill; I will make a good act of contrition and will assure my salvation in that way." No, no, that is an error.[3]

In reality, who knows if I will not again commit some mortal sin? Who knows if, brought before a tribunal and asked to renounce my faith, I may not be a renegade? That happens to him who little by little becomes careless.[4]

Reflection

A retreat purifies the soul from sin.

Sin is an insult of the creature to its Creator.

You must give this truth your attentive consideration.

You are a sinner. We all are sinners. Only the Immaculate Virgin was conceived without sin and never committed any personal sins. Today, people don't want to hear about sin. It's considered antiquated, medieval, hateful, and meaningless. Ironically, it's most often the people who don't like to hear about sin who consider themselves immaculate and free of sin. Have you ever noticed how so few people stand in line for Confession and yet almost everyone gets in line to receive Holy Communion? Is everyone free of serious sin? Is everyone immaculate?

In 1946, Venerable Pope Pius XII stated, "Perhaps the greatest sin in the world today is that men have begun to lose the sense of sin."[5] Catholics have been so poorly catechized in recent decades that they don't even know what sin is or that it greatly offends God's love. They have not been taught that sin tarnishes a soul, harming its relationship with God and others. Our Retreat Master notes, "Sin is something foul, corrupt, and putrid. It disfigures our souls — especially sins of sensuality — and we are visible to God in that state!"[6] God doesn't want to see us in that state. He wants to see us living in a state of sanctifying grace.

To love God and live a life pleasing to him, you need to know how to receive the medicine of mercy properly. In God's plan, there is an order to his mercy and an order to how he dispenses it. Without a doubt, God is free to dispense his mercy as he sees fit, but according to how he has revealed himself to us in Divine Revelation, he has most definitely established a norm and an order for the distribution of his mercy. The norm for the distribution of his mercy comes to us through the Sacraments of Confession and Holy Communion. However, the order of receiving these sacraments of mercy (Holy Communion and Confession) is not the same for each sinner. Those who have committed lesser (venial) sins continue to be in a state of sanctifying grace and have a different order for receiving mercy than those who have committed serious (mortal) sins because by gravely sinning they have placed themselves outside of sanctifying grace.

God wants all to receive the medicine of mercy through Confession and Holy Communion, but Confession must come first for those who are in mortal sin. Otherwise, the application of the medicine is ineffective, even harmful to the soul. The proper order of mercy for the person who has fallen into mortal sin is to go to Confession before receiving Holy Communion. Without Confession, people in mortal sin who receive Holy Communion make the wound worse because they are committing a sacrilegious act by receiving Holy Communion in a state of mortal sin.

For the person who falls and commits venial sins, the application of the medicine of mercy has a different order. Such persons may receive Holy Communion without going to Confession first. The Church only requires that those aware of venial sin go to Confession once a year. The reason the Church only requires Confession once a year for those who commit venial sins is because the Penitential Rite at the beginning of Holy Mass takes away venial sins.

Don't you want to go to Confession more than once a year, though? Don't you want to express your love for God by examining yourself and turning away from any and all sin? Do you bathe more than once a year? Do you brush your teeth or do laundry more than once a year? Sure you do. Isn't your soul more important than your body? Again, according to the legislation of the Church, you only have to go to Confession once a year if you are only aware that you committed venial sins, but you have been called to follow more than laws. You have been called to pursue and follow divine love. Therefore, it is a very good practice to go to Confession on a regular basis, even if you have only committed venial sins. It's why children go to Confession before receiving First Holy Communion. Children preparing to receive First Holy Communion are most likely not guilty of falling into mortal sin. "First Reconciliation," as it is often called, is meant to teach children that Confession is akin to getting a tune-up for your soul, the engine of your being. The soul runs a lot smoother when it receives regular maintenance. It's never a good idea to wait until the engine of your being (your soul) needs a complete overhaul, which is what happens when you fall into mortal sin. Maintain it by a frequent tune-up (frequent Confession).

Holy Communion and Confession work together for the good of the soul. This is why any Eucharistic revival that doesn't concomitantly promote a revival of the Sacrament of Reconciliation (Confession) will not bear lasting fruit. Repentance and the Heavenly Manna are a package deal. You can't have one without the other. All the saints understood this. They knew that being free of serious sin and receiving the Eucharist give you the ability to advance quickly in the spiritual life and be transformed by the supernatural effects of the Blessed Sacrament. Confession and the Eucharist give you the ability to be "transubstantiated" into a saint!

> I began to amend my life by frequenting Holy Communion after having tried every other way and failed. When I went rarely to Holy Communion, I had no end of bad habits and imperfections that appeared to me insurmountable. I uprooted these by multiplying my Communions.[7]
>
> — St. Claude de la Colombière

No saint would ever receive Holy Communion in a state of mortal sin, believing that by doing so they would experience healing, growth in holiness, and closeness to God. Such thinking is theological nonsense and extremely dangerous to a soul. Saints know that receiving Holy Communion only in a state of grace is what truly brings a person closer to God and closer to sanctity. Our Retreat Master instructs us, "The greatest saints are really persuaded that they are great sinners, and they say so because they think so. We consider this exaggerated and say that they could not possibly believe it. And yet they are really convinced that they are the greatest sinners before God, because they have true humility and patience, which are the means of knowing one's wretchedness thoroughly."[8]

What about you? When is the last time you went to Confession? An honest, hold-nothing-back Confession? You need to do it, and you need to do it sometime before the end of this retreat. Do not put it off. Don't you want to be a saint? Don't you want to go to heaven?

Reflection Questions

1. Why does sin displease God more than anything?
2. What are those sins and attachments that keep you from truly loving God?
3. What are some practical steps you can take to remove sin in your life?

Resolution

Today, place yourself spiritually before the Blessed Sacrament, asking the Holy Spirit to reveal your sins and disordered attachments. Make a promise to Jesus to go to Confession soon, sometime before the end of this retreat.

Prayer

Dear Jesus, my Eucharistic Lord, I ask pardon for every sin I have ever committed. I never want to separate myself from you. I love you and thank you for loving me and being merciful to me. Help me to make a good, thorough confession in the Sacrament of Reconciliation. Our Lady of the Most Blessed Sacrament, teach me to abhor sin and love God so much that I never want to displease him again through actions that are displeasing to him. Saint Joseph, help me to wage a holy war against sin and give me the courage to root out anything in my life that is offensive to Jesus. Saint Peter Julian Eymard, Apostle of the Eucharist, fill me with your Eucharistic zeal so that I might love the Blessed Sacrament above all things.

Pray the Litany of the Holy Eucharist (page 163)

DAY 6
Unworthiness

Perhaps the sense of your unworthiness keeps you away from this God of all sanctity? It is true that the greatest saint, or even the purest of the Cherubim, is unworthy to receive the divine Host, but do you not see that Jesus is hiding his virtues, is hiding his very sanctity, to show you his goodness simply and solely? Do you not hear that sweet voice inviting you: "Come unto me"? Do you not feel the nearness of that divine love like a magnet drawing you? After all, it is not your merits which give you your rights, nor is it your virtues which open to you the doors of the Cenacle; it is the love of Jesus.[1]

Perhaps the greatness of God overwhelms your nothingness. It should not. This heavenly and divine greatness which rules in Heaven does not exist in Communion. Do you not see how Jesus has disguised himself that you may not be frightened and may be bold enough to look at him and come near him?[2]

But I may be guilty of sins! If, after examining yourself, you have not the moral certainty, the positive knowledge of a mortal sin, you may go to Holy Communion.

Let not vain pretexts, therefore, keep you away from the altar rail. Live in such a way as to be admitted frequently and even daily to fruitful Communions. Become more perfect so as to communicate well, and live in such a way as to communicate often.[3]

The Eucharist is a bread of delights. The first condition to partake of it is to be alive, that is, in the state of grace. That is the first and only essential condition: freedom from mortal sin. Of course it is only proper that we should also be without venial sins and have some piety and virtues. But the general law, indispensable and for everybody, is to be free from mortal sin.[4]

Reflection

It is not your merits that give you your rights. It is the love of Jesus.

Jesus has disguised himself that you may not be frightened.

The Eucharist is a bread of delights!

Do you feel unworthy to receive Holy Communion? You should. You are unworthy. We are all unworthy. Knowing your unworthiness is a sign that you have a healthy spiritual life and a proper disposition for receiving Holy Communion. Even the Virgin Mary knew she was unworthy to receive her Divine Son in Holy Communion. What a sight that must have been when St. John the Apostle, St. Peter, or one of the other apostles gave Holy Communion to Our Lady! How privileged the Apostles were to see in what manner and how reverently the Blessed Mother received Holy Communion.

Though we are all unworthy of such a great gift, our Retreat Master is very clear that the only thing that should keep us from Holy Communion is mortal sin. Sometimes people suffer from scrupulosity and irrational fears, and they refrain from receiving the Holy Eucharist. Struggles such as these should be shared with a wise spiritual director who can offer guidance and help in these matters. What is important is that a person has a clear and well-formed conscience, a conscience informed and guided by natural law, divine law, and the teachings of the Catholic Church. Jesus yearns to be united with us in Holy Communion. We will never be worthy, but we should do everything in our power to receive him as often as possible.

The effects of frequent Holy Communion are tremendous. Our Retreat Master notes, "We can never encourage frequent Communion too strongly. It is not an abuse. Is it an abuse for a child to visit its father and keep near him? It is the same with one of the faithful who seeks frequent Communion with our Lord."[5] The fire of Divine Love is waiting to consume you, to take your weaknesses and clothe you with strength. Frequent Holy Communion is a secret to sanctity.

The more you love God, the more you will want him to eradicate sin out of your life. Nothing separates you from God but mortal sin. If you repent and go to Confession, he is always ready to take you back. Our Retreat Master states, "Communion, received frequently and with the requisite dispositions, is the surest pledge of eternal salvation."[6] Eternal life begins now with Holy Communion. To a religious sister, our Retreat Master once wrote, "Yes, receive Communion as often as he [the priest] permits. You need it. You tell me that you are not worthy of it. That's true, the angels are not worthy of it. All the holiness we could have doesn't make us deserving of a single Communion in our whole life."[7]

Jesus did not die on the Cross to remain in the tabernacle. He died to dwell in your soul and be received by you in Holy Communion. He wants his Sacred Heart in the Eucharist to replace your stony heart. According to the laws of the Church, you are obligated as a Catholic to attend Holy Mass every Sunday and Holy Day of Obligation, yet only required to receive Jesus in Holy Communion once a year. Yet don't you want to receive him more than once a year? The Church allows you to receive Holy Communion every day. Wouldn't it be a sign of a pitiful friendship with Jesus only to receive Holy Communion once a year? If you are not in mortal sin, why would you not receive him weekly, even daily? If you are madly in love with Jesus, as he is madly in love with you, why would you not receive him as often as possible? Saints of old would be spiritually jealous of your ability to receive him daily since the ability of the faithful to receive Holy Communion daily only became common practice in modern times. It wasn't until the early 20th century that the laity were allowed to receive Holy Communion on a daily basis. You live in a privileged time. Take advantage of it! Don't miss the grace!

> Do you suffer from pride? Receive the Eucharist, that is, Christ humbling himself down to the flesh, indeed down to bread, and this humble bread will make you humble. Are you afflicted with the temptation of lust? Receive the wine that generates virgins. Are you afflicted with anger and impatience? Receive Christ crucified, the most patient, and he will give you a share in his patience.[8]

— St. Stanislaus Papczyński

Reflection Questions

1. How can your sense of unworthiness be a means to sanctity?
2. Do you experience fears or scrupulosity about receiving Holy Communion?
3. Have you ever attended Holy Mass on a weekday? Have you thought about attending Holy Mass daily?

Resolution

Today, ask Our Lady for the grace to receive her Eucharistic Son with greater confidence, humility, and love. Promise never to receive Holy Communion in a state of mortal sin.

Prayer

Dear Jesus, my Eucharistic Lord, though I am unworthy to receive you, let nothing but mortal sin keep me from receiving you. I stand as a beggar before you. Help me to never forget how much you love me. Our Lady of the Most Blessed Sacrament, give me your pure heart so that my heart may be a fitting dwelling place for our Eucharistic Lord. Saint Joseph, help me to treasure every reception of Holy Communion. Saint Peter Julian Eymard, Apostle of the Eucharist, fill me

with your Eucharistic zeal so that I might love the Blessed
Sacrament above all things.

Pray the Litany of the Most Precious Blood (page 166)

DAY 7
The Mercy of God

Retreat Master: St. Peter Julian Eymard

God's mercy is magnanimous. He pardons generously and forever, for he knows not how to forget only half. He restores the joy of innocence and the honor of the first state. He pardons not as a man, but as God. He wishes us still to remember our sins, but with a thought of love, of gratitude, in order to laud his mercy which has pardoned them.[1]

Believe me, then, live always of the mercy of God. Let me suppose that you have never committed sin. What has preserved you? Mercy, the same that reclaimed me, a sinner. We are debtors to this Divine Mercy. Live also on gratitude toward it, and place all your trust in it.

If the good God were not infinite in mercy, if he did not know that it could never be exhausted, however great the floods of it that he constantly pours out, he never would have undertaken to lead us to paradise. How many preventing graces to give, how many falls to repair, how many long-suffering pardons, what innumerable pardons during a man's lifetime! The good God is never discouraged. His mercy never abandons us, and at our last sigh, it is there to receive us.[2]

Everyone knows how much he owes to the mercy of God, and we can all say that it is due to him that we have not fallen into hell. The more sins we have committed, the more grateful should we be to his mercy.[3]

Reflection

Live always of the mercy of God!
Place all your trust in it.
His mercy never abandons us.

The Holy Eucharist is an ocean of mercy. If you have been to the ocean, you probably noticed that the crashing waves never stop. They are endless. So it is with the mercy of God and his love for us in the Blessed Sacrament. When you gaze upon the Sacred Host, you are gazing upon the infinite mercy of God. The Eucharist is the supreme proof of God's love and mercy. In the Blessed Sacrament, the God of mercy awaits us and beckons us, so that he might shower us with mercy at Holy Mass and in adoration. The Eucharist is Divine Mercy because the Eucharist is Jesus Christ, Mercy Incarnate.

In Eucharistic adoration, you see the humble and merciful God who draws you to himself in order for you to receive his love and mercy. The same Lord who forgave St. Mary Magdalene, St. Peter, persecutors, and executioners wants to pour mercy into your soul in the Blessed Sacrament. He waits for you night and day in the tabernacle, wanting to heal you, forgive you, strengthen you, and above all, love you. From the tabernacle, he gazes upon you with the gaze of mercy. He beckons you to approach him and spend time with him. Like the father in the story of the prodigal son, Jesus runs to us with his merciful love and Eucharistic heart.

The Divine Mercy message and devotion given by God to the world through St. Faustina Kowalska is a gift for our times. Interestingly, not many people know that St. Faustina's full name in religious life was Sr. Maria Faustina Kowalska of the Blessed Sacrament of the Congregation of Sisters of Our Lady of Mercy. Mary, mercy, and the Eucharist. She had it all!

On one occasion Jesus said to St. Faustina,

Oh, how painful it is to me that souls so seldom unite themselves to me in Holy Communion. I wait for souls, and they are indifferent toward me. I love them tenderly and sincerely, and they distrust me. I want to lavish my graces on them, and they do not want to accept them. They treat me as a dead object, whereas my heart is full of love and mercy.[4]

How sad. Jesus wants to be united to us but so often Catholics treat the Sacred Host as a dead object. It is not a dead object but the living God! Jesus is living and fully present in the Blessed Sacrament. What he wants from us is trust. We must trust in Divine Mercy and trust that Jesus is truly present in the Eucharist. When Jesus instructed St. Faustina to have an image painted of his Divine Mercy, he informed her that the words "Jesus, I trust in you" were to be written at the bottom of the image. In a certain sense, the Divine Mercy image is an icon of the Holy Eucharist. When we gaze upon the Divine Mercy image, we behold the blood and water flowing from the pierced heart of Jesus. When we gaze upon the Blessed Sacrament in Eucharistic adoration, the blood and water that poured forth from the heart of Jesus truly permeate us like rays, flooding our souls with mercy. Our role is to trust.

Before the Holy Eucharist, we are recipients of Divine Mercy. We owe everything to the infinite mercy of God. Every time you come before the Eucharistic presence of Jesus in adoration or receive him in Holy Communion, you receive his mercy. The Chaplet of the Divine Mercy is itself a deeply Eucharistic prayer:

> Eternal Father, I offer you the Body, Blood, Soul, and Divinity of your dearly beloved Son, Our Lord Jesus Christ, in atonement for our sins and those of the whole world. For the sake of his sorrowful Passion, have mercy on us and on the whole world. ...

The Eucharistic heart of Jesus beats with love and mercy for you. His Eucharistic heart wants to save you from the fires of hell and lead you to the shores of paradise. Trust him.

Reflection Questions

1. How has God's mercy, especially for your past sins, led you to gratitude?
2. Have you personally experienced the mercy of God in Eucharistic adoration or Holy Communion?
3. How can you grow in trust of God's mercy?

Resolution

Today, make an act of trust in God's mercy. Let go of the past, the present, and the future. Abandon all to mercy. Repeat throughout the day, "Jesus, I trust in you!"

Prayer

Dear Jesus, my Eucharistic Lord, I trust in you. I abandon myself completely to you. Give me great confidence in your mercy and help me never to doubt you. You are all worthy of my love, and I ask you to forgive me for the times I have lacked confidence in your love and mercy. Our Lady of the Most Blessed Sacrament, Mother of Mercy, help me to place all my trust in your Son's Eucharistic heart. Saint Joseph, help me to be a vessel of trust. Saint Peter Julian Eymard, Apostle of the Eucharist, fill me with your Eucharistic zeal so that I might love the Blessed Sacrament above all things.

Pray the Litany of the Holy Eucharist (page 163)

DAY 8
The Devil and the Holy Eucharist

Retreat Master: St. Peter Julian Eymard

The devil wages incessant warfare on our love for Jesus in the Most Blessed Sacrament. He knows that Jesus is there, living and substantially present; that by himself he [Jesus] is drawing souls and taking direct possession of them. The devil tries to efface the thought of the Eucharist in us, and the good impression made by it; for in his mind, that should decide the issue of the struggle. And yet God is all love.[1]

The devil seems triumphant; he mocks Jesus. "I give man nothing that is true, good, or beautiful," he says. "I have not suffered for his sake, and I am more loved, more obeyed, and better served than thou."[2]

Oh! How well the devil knows that by keeping souls away from the Eucharist he is destroying the Christian family and fostering selfishness in us. For there are only two loves: the love of God and the love of self. We must give ourselves to the one or to the other.[3]

How unhappy are they who no longer have the Eucharist! What darkness! What lawlessness of mind! What coldness of heart! Satan alone reigns as master and with him every evil passion! As for us, the Eucharist delivers us from all evils![4]

Reflection

The devil wages incessant warfare on our love for Jesus in the Most Blessed Sacrament.

The devil tries to efface the thought of the Eucharist in us.

How unhappy are they who no longer have the Eucharist!

Can you imagine what life would be like without the Eucharist? It's a frightening thought. God would seem aloof, distant, and far away. Living without Jesus in the tabernacle would feel lonely and empty. This is why knowing that the Real Presence is in the tabernacle changes everything in life. His Real Presence gives meaning to our days, fills our hearts with joy and hope, and gives peace of mind in the midst of a fallen world. It's no wonder the devil wants to separate you from the Eucharist.

While the devil definitely wants you to sin and offend God and his love, the devil knows well that the only thing that can bring you true happiness in this life, and everlasting joy in the next, is the Holy Eucharist. It is for this reason that the devil's primary tactic of bringing souls to ruin is to estrange them from the Eucharist. The Eucharist is the key to happiness and true life in God. The devil doesn't want you to go to heaven. He wants you to go to hell.

The devil knows that if he can get you to doubt the Real Presence, it is very likely that you will eventually fall away from believing in sin, hell, and the devil himself. He knows that to walk away from the Eucharist is to walk away from life. To abandon belief in the Real Presence of Jesus in the Eucharist is to lack trust in God's merciful love and plan for your salvation. The devil does not want you to trust God. Something every Christian needs to know is that Jesus meant what he said when he taught his apostles and disciples about his Real Presence in the Eucharist. Regarding this, did you know that in the New Testament there is only one book that has 66 verses in the sixth chapter? It's John 6:66. Everybody knows that 666 is associated with the devil and the number of the beast. So what is John 6:66 about? Lack of belief in the Eucharist!

Read it yourself:

v. 48 "I am the bread of life.
v. 49 Your ancestors ate the manna in the desert,
but they died;
v. 50 this is the bread that comes down from

heaven so that one may eat it and not die.

v. 51 I am the living bread that came down from heaven; whoever eats this bread will live forever; and the bread that I will give is my flesh for the life of the world."

v. 52 The Jews quarreled among themselves, saying, "How can this man give us his flesh to eat?"

v. 53 Jesus said to them, "Amen, amen, I say to you, unless you eat the flesh of the Son of Man and drink his blood, you do not have life within you.

v. 54 Whoever eats my flesh and drinks my blood has eternal life, and I will raise him on the last day.

v. 55 For my flesh is true food, and my blood is true drink.

v. 56 Whoever eats my flesh and drinks my blood remains in me and I in him.

v. 57 Just as the living Father sent me and I have life because of the Father, so also the one who feeds on me will have life because of me.

v. 58 This is the bread that came down from heaven. Unlike your ancestors who ate and still died, whoever eats this bread will live forever."

v. 59 These things he said while teaching in the synagogue in Capernaum.

v. 60 Then many of his disciples who were listening said, "This saying is hard; who can accept it?"

v. 61 Since Jesus knew that his disciples were murmuring about this, he said to them, "Does this shock you?

v. 62 What if you were to see the Son of Man ascending to where he was before?

v. 63 It is the spirit that gives life, while the flesh is of no avail. The words I have spoken to you are spirit and life.

v. 64 But there are some of you who do not believe." Jesus knew from the beginning the ones who would not believe and the one who would betray him.

v. 65 And he said, "For this reason I have told you that no one can come to me unless it is granted him by my Father."

v. 66 As a result of this, many of his disciples returned to their former way of life and no longer accompanied him.

That's an eye-opener! The devil launched his assault on belief in the Real Presence by instilling in the minds and hearts of Jesus' first disciples doubts about his vital (life-giving) teaching on the Eucharist. The evil one has been instilling doubts in the minds of Jesus' disciples ever since. The devil knows that Jesus is the Bread of Life and truly present in the Eucharist; he doesn't want you to know it. When you accept and trust this teaching of Jesus, you have the key to freedom.

Prior to the so-called Protestant Reformation, all Christians believed in the Real Presence of Jesus in Holy Communion. Sadly, after the Protestant Reformation, Christian sects began to teach different understandings of the presence of Jesus in Holy Communion — basically John 6:66 all over again. Many followers of Jesus began to say that Jesus only meant it as a symbol, not to be taken literally. Others began to say that Jesus was somehow present when the Eucharist was celebrated but did not remain with or in Holy Communion once church was over. Yet, to this day, it's only Catholic churches that Satanists seek to steal a Sacred Host from when they want to desecrate and commit sacrilege against God. Why is this? Well, even the devil knows where Jesus is truly present in the Eucharist. The devil knows it's in the Catholic

Church.[5] Devil worshipers don't steal communion hosts from Methodist churches, Lutheran churches, or any other group. Only Catholic churches.

The devil hates belief in the Eucharist because belief in the Real Presence is a constant reminder to the devil of just how much God loves mankind. Every Holy Communion received in a state of grace torments the devil. It loosens his grip and sets souls free. Our Retreat Master states, "In the Holy Eucharist, Jesus still manifests his power over demons. When in exorcisms, in order to conquer the demons that have resisted all other means, the Sacred Host has been presented to them, they have uttered cries of rage, and succumbed to their God present."[6]

So powerful is the Eucharist against the devil that our Retreat Master once made the following statement: "The reign of the devil returns in proportion to the lessening of faith in the Eucharist."[7] As for you, turn away from the lies of the devil and his desire for you to doubt the Real Presence. Make reparation for those who do not believe, do not adore, do not trust, and do not love Jesus in the Eucharist. Shame the devil and pray for a revival of belief in the Eucharist in your own heart and in the hearts of people around the world.

> The Eucharist is a fire which inflames us, that, like lions breathing fire, we may retire from the altar made terrible to the devil.[8]
>
> — St. John Chrysostom

Reflection Questions

1. Why does the devil wage continuous warfare against the Holy Eucharist?

2. How does the devil try to weaken your faith in the Real Presence?

3. How does the Eucharist help you conquer sin, the devil, and the world?

Resolution

Today, renounce the devil and his desire to take you away from the Blessed Sacrament. Profess your belief and make an act of trust in the Real Presence. Pray for a revival of belief in the Real Presence.

Prayer

Dear Jesus, my Eucharistic Lord, have pity on me for the times I have allowed the devil to distract me and make me doubt your teaching on the Eucharist. Forgive me for any time I have received you unworthily. Forgive me for never visiting you in the Blessed Sacrament. Our Lady of the Most Blessed Sacrament, I beg you to bring back those who have fallen away from belief in the Real Presence of your Son. Saint Joseph, Terror of Demons, protect us from the devil, and give us a Eucharistic faith that conquers all doubt and darkness. Saint Peter Julian Eymard, Apostle of the Eucharist, fill me with your Eucharistic zeal so that I might love the Blessed Sacrament above all things.

Pray the Litany of the Most Precious Blood (page 166)

DAY 9
Reparation

Retreat Master: St. Peter Julian Eymard

We see Christians despise Jesus in the Most Blessed Sacrament and his heart which has so loved them and which consumes itself with love for them! To despise him, they take advantage of the veil which hides him! They insult him with their irreverences.[1]

In his agony he sought a consoler; on the Cross he asked for someone to sympathize with his afflictions. Today more than ever, we must make amends, a reparation of honor, to the adorable heart of Jesus. Let us lavish adorations, our love on the Eucharist. To the heart of Jesus living in the most Blessed Sacrament be honor, praise, adoration, kingly power forever and ever![2]

Strive to become a victim of reparation for so much indifference, so many sacrileges against Jesus Eucharistic. It is the work for our times. Great evils require great remedies.[3]

This is your mission, O adorers: to weep at the feet of Jesus despised by his own, crucified in so many hearts and abandoned in so many places.[4]

Reflection

Today more than ever, we must make amends.

Great evils require great remedies.

This is your mission, O adorers.

It is heartbreaking to think that there are people who intentionally blaspheme and desecrate the Holy Eucharist. It is even more heartbreaking when those who claim to be followers of Jesus offend him and commit sacrilege against the Blessed Sacrament.

Who of us is ignorant of the countless outrages done the Catholic religion and of the unheard-of blasphemies of which its adorable author is the constant object in many parts of the world? Christ and his religion are outraged by forgetfulness of evangelical truths and abandonment of the sacraments.

The Church is outraged by the vast plan of persecution hatched for many years and in many countries against bishops and priests. Religion is outraged by the battering down of crosses and the profanation of churches.

> Worse than these outrages, from those who have never been of the true fold and who have grown up in the abuse of grace and that almost universal hardness of heart so characteristic of this genera-tion, are the outrages of hypocritical sinners who go to Communion unworthily and sacrilegiously.[5]
>
> — Blessed Basil Moreau

Strong words, but Blessed Basil Moreau is right. People, especially Catholics, need to hear such words today. Politi-cians and public figures — many of whom openly profess to be devout Catholics — who support abortion and so-called homosexual marriage should not be receiving Holy Com-munion. They need to go to Confession and repent publicly. Saint Paul warned the early Christians about these matters:

> For as often as you eat this bread and drink the cup, you proclaim the death of the Lord until he comes. Therefore whoever eats the bread or drinks the cup of the Lord unworthily will have to answer for the body and blood of the Lord. A person should examine himself, and so eat the bread and drink the cup. For anyone who eats and drinks without discerning the body, eats and drinks judgment on himself. That is why many among you are ill and infirm, and a considerable number are dying. (1 Corinthians 11:26–30)

The reception of Holy Communion by those living in and promoting immoral lifestyles is an abomination and causes grave scandal to the faithful. The pope, bishops, cardinals, priests, and deacons should be preaching on these issues and correcting these errors. It must be done with love, but it must be done. Yet, today, many in the hierarchy do nothing to correct these abuses and offenses against our Eucharistic Lord, or even worse, they themselves openly advocate that all Catholics, regardless of their lifestyle and promotion of evil, should be given Holy Communion. What has become of so many in the leadership of the Catholic Church? Have they not read the New Testament and the lives of the saints? Do they truly know and love Jesus Christ? Do they love souls and want them to go to heaven? Has the leadership of the Church forgotten that admonishing sinners and calling the wayward to repentance is a work of mercy?

To make reparation to the Eucharistic heart of Jesus is the work of our times. When hatred, indifference, and sacrilegious reception of the Holy Eucharist increases, our reparation must increase. When we make reparation for the many offenses against the Blessed Sacrament, we console Jesus and offer him our hearts full of love and gratitude for his Real Presence in the Eucharist. If someone abused, blasphemed, bullied, or maligned your friend, wouldn't you stand up for your friend, letting him know that he is loved, and shower him with kind words and love? Shouldn't we do the same for Jesus, our best friend?

> The virtue of gratitude obliges us to make reparation, insofar as we can, for the shameful treatment received by the Body of the Savior.[6]
>
> — Blessed Basil Moreau

Making reparation to our Eucharistic Lord can be as simple as saying a short prayer. At Fatima, an angel knelt alongside the three children, instructing them to recite the following prayer three times:

Most Holy Trinity, Father, Son and Holy Spirit,
I adore you profoundly, and I offer you the Most
Precious Body, Blood, Soul and Divinity of Jesus
Christ, present in all the tabernacles of the world,
in reparation for the outrages, sacrileges and indifference with which he himself is offended. And,
through the infinite merits of his Most Sacred
Heart, and the Immaculate Heart of Mary, I beg
of you the conversion of poor sinners.[7]

What about you? What are you going to do when
our Eucharistic Lord is so offended and maligned in Holy
Communion? Make it your mission to console him and make
reparation to his love.

Reflection Questions
1. Have you committed any offenses against the
   Holy Eucharist?
2. What are some ways that people offend the
   Blessed Sacrament?
3. How can you make reparation to our Eucharistic
   Lord?

Resolution
Today, make an act of reparation to the Blessed Sacrament.
Let Jesus know that you love him and are sorry for anything
you and others have done that has offended his Real Presence
in the Eucharist.

Prayer
Dear Jesus, my Eucharistic Lord, have mercy on me for the
times I have offended you in the Blessed Sacrament. I love
you and want others to love you. Please have mercy on all
who have offended you. Our Lady of the Most Blessed Sacrament, help me to console Jesus and make reparation to his
Eucharistic heart. Saint Joseph, I want to love Jesus in the
Eucharist more than I ever have before. Saint Peter Julian

Eymard, Apostle of the Eucharist, fill me with your Eucharistic zeal so that I might love the Blessed Sacrament above all things.

Pray the Litany of the Holy Eucharist (page 163)

DAY 10
Prayer and Holiness

Retreat Master: St. Peter Julian Eymard

Prayer is the distinguishing characteristic of the Catholic religion; it is the sign of a soul's holiness; indeed, it is its holiness. It both makes holy and is the first evidence of holiness. When you see someone living a life of prayer, you may say: "There goes a saint!"

Saint Paul, having heard the call of God, immediately began to pray. And what did he do for three days at Damascus? He prayed. And when the priest Ananias, in spite of the divine command, hesitated to go to this persecutor of the Christians to baptize him, the Lord said to him: "Go, you will find him praying." That is, he is already a saint, for he prays. The Lord did not say: "He is mortifying himself, he is fasting," but, "He is praying." Every soul that prays will attain holiness.[1]

Prayer is, then, man's greatest glorification of God. Prayer is man's greatest virtue. It is a combination of all the virtues, because they all prepare it and compose it. Prayer is faith believing, hope supplicating, love demanding. Prayer is the humility of heart that formulates it, the confidence that utters it, and the perseverance which triumphs over God himself!

Eucharistic prayer has a still higher excellence. Like a fiery dart it rises directly to the heart of God.[2]

Reflection

Every soul that prays will attain holiness.

Prayer is faith believing, hope supplicating, love demanding.

Eucharistic prayer rises directly to the heart of God.

What about you? Do you pray? Do you have a Eucharistic prayer life?

Prayer is absolutely necessary if you want to become a saint. Some saints are known for their humility and service to the poor, others for their fortitude and courage, while others for their hiddenness and penitential lives. What makes each saint like the others is that they all prayed. Prayer enabled all of them to live lives of heroic virtue. Without prayer, it is impossible to be holy. And persevering in prayer is essential. Prayer is not always going to feel wonderful or pleasant, because prayer is not about feelings or emotions. Prayer is about love. Love perseveres.

Most Christians would agree that prayer is essential to growing closer to God and increasing in virtue. Yet so many Christians find it difficult to persevere in prayer. We are easily distracted, only praying before meals or before going to bed. We come up with all sorts of excuses for not making prayer a vital part of our daily life. But if we don't pray, we are headed for trouble. Prayer is not an option.

Acquiring a Eucharist-centered prayer life makes prayer easier for a person and gives you a greater ability to persevere in it. When you make the Eucharist the center of your daily work and actions, your prayer life becomes a part of your being.

Let's unpack what is meant by having a Eucharistic-centered prayer life.

When you are in your home, you most likely know in which direction the nearest hospital is located. You know in what direction any and all important places are located, no matter what room you are in in the house. Were you to go outside you would know what direction you would need to travel in to get to these places. We all have an interior compass for the most important things and places in our life. We especially know in what direction family and friends live, as well church, work, school, the grocery store, post office, and police station.

What about the Real Presence of Jesus in the tabernacle? Isn't Jesus the most important person in your life? As a

Catholic, you should know where the nearest tabernacle is in relation to your home or wherever you are at the moment. Saints have an interior Eucharistic compass. They always know where the nearest church and tabernacle are located. Such a Eucharistic-centered life will change your life, especially your prayer life. As the Sun is the center of our solar system, with the Earth, moon, and all the other planets revolving around it, the Eucharist should be the center of your day with all other things revolving around it.

> The presence of Jesus in the tabernacle must be a kind of magnetic pole attracting an ever greater number of souls enamored of him, ready to wait patiently to hear his voice and, as it were, to sense the beating of his heart.[3]
>
> — Pope St. John Paul II

> The tabernacle must become everyone's home, everyone's residence, a place where people meet, the point of reference, the parameter, the unit of measurement.[4]
>
> — Blessed Carlo Acutis

As humans, we need points of reference to keep us on track. Having points of reference in life helps you stay on course so that you are not wandering endlessly and always getting lost. Jesus provides the same thing for you in the Blessed Sacrament. It doesn't matter if the nearest tabernacle is 10 miles from your home or one mile away. Likewise, it doesn't matter if the nearest tabernacle to your workplace is 4 miles away or 20 miles away. For God there is no distance. Your genuflection before the tabernacle is recognized by God whether you are in church and only several feet away from the Real Presence, or if you are 20 miles away and genuflecting to the tabernacle from your bedroom.

When you become aware of the location of the Real Presence of Jesus in the tabernacle at all times, and center all your daily routine around the Blessed Sacrament, prayer becomes second nature. It no longer feels forced or burdensome. You are always in church because your heart, mind, and soul are always united and directed toward the Real Presence in the tabernacle. No matter where you are, you are before Jesus. Yes, the ability to attend daily Mass and adore the Blessed Sacrament is a great blessing, but the majority of people find it difficult to do on a daily basis because of work, family life, and daily responsibilities. Yet everyone can center their life around Jesus in the tabernacle and have the ability to pray at all times, no matter where they are. You can do it too!

Once you know in what direction the nearest tabernacle is to your location, your being becomes Eucharistic and your prayer life becomes Eucharistic. You know where his Real Presence is no matter where you are at any given moment. All your acts of piety and devotion are directed toward the Blessed Sacrament. When you wake up in the morning, you are able to face the direction of the tabernacle, genuflect, and say a prayer. It doesn't require pinpoint accuracy and exact longitude and latitude coordinates either. At work, study, or times of recreation and leisure, you can do the same. A Eucharistic-centered life gives you the ability to praise him, thank him, adore him, and say a prayer for family and friends with your interior Eucharistic compass on. Living this kind of Eucharistic-centered spirituality changes everything. It's that easy!

> Visiting the tabernacle means making oneself a candidate for holiness.[5]
>
> — Blessed Carlo Acutis

> Prayer made in union with this divine sacrifice has untold power.[6]
>
> — St. Francis de Sales

Nowhere does Jesus hear our prayers more readily than in the Blessed Sacrament.[7]

— Blessed Henry Suso

Reflection Questions

1. What is your understanding of prayer?
2. Do you have a Eucharistic-centered prayer life?
3. What can you do to have an interior Eucharistic compass?

Resolution

Today, no matter where you are, place yourself in the presence of the Blessed Sacrament, remembering that distance is not an obstacle. Tell Jesus you are grateful for his presence in the tabernacle. Make a decision to start living a Eucharistic-centered prayer life.

Prayer

Dear Jesus, my Eucharistic Lord, thank you for giving me the grace to pray. Forgive me for the times when my prayer has been distracted and selfish. Teach me how to pray like a saint and orient me always toward your Real Presence. Our Lady of the Most Blessed Sacrament, intercede before the Eucharist for me, and grant me the grace to pray like you. Saint Joseph, help me to live a Eucharistic-centered life. Saint Peter Julian Eymard, Apostle of the Eucharist, fill me with your Eucharistic zeal so that I might love the Blessed Sacrament above all things.

Pray the Litany of the Most Precious Blood (page 166)

DAY 11
Eucharistic Faith

Retreat Master: St. Peter Julian Eymard

The Eucharistic veil perfects our faith. Faith is a pure act of the mind, disengaged from the senses. Here the senses are not brought into play, they have no action. It is the only mystery of Jesus Christ in which the senses have to keep absolute silence. In all the others, in the Incarnation, the Redemption, they behold an infant God, a dying God. In this mystery nothing is presented to them but an impenetrable veil. Here, faith alone must act. The Eucharist is the kingdom of faith.

This Eucharistic cloud demands from us a very meritorious sacrifice, that of our mind and our reason. We must believe even against the evidence of our senses, against the ordinary laws of existence, against our own experience. We must believe on the simple word of Jesus Christ. There is only one question to be asked: "Who is there?"—"I" responds Jesus Christ. Let us fall down and adore!

And this pure faith, disengaged from the senses, free in its action, brings us in closest union with Jesus Christ in the Most Blessed Sacrament. The soul clears the barrier of the senses and enters into the admirable contemplation of the divine presence of God under the Sacred Species.

Ah, yes! It was only the wisdom and goodness of our Lord that could invent the Eucharistic veil![1]

Reflection

The Eucharistic veil perfects our faith.

The Eucharist is the kingdom of faith.

Let us fall down and adore!

Belief in the Real Presence of Jesus Christ in the Holy

Eucharist — Body, Blood, Soul, and Divinity — requires tremendous faith. The Almighty God who took on human nature, humbling himself to be placed in a crib, walk among us, and be crucified on the Cross is now hidden by the veil of a piece of bread. To the person of faith, the Eucharist is the Alpha and the Omega, the source and summit of life itself. How incredible the Eucharistic mystery! How humble and marvelous to possess the gift of faith!

Faith, the theological virtue by which we firmly believe everything God has revealed to us to be true, is on full display when someone believes in the Real Presence of Jesus in Holy Communion. This kind of extraordinary faith, faith that goes beyond what our own five senses can tell us, is so amazing that Jesus calls those who have it blessed.

> Thomas, called Didymus, one of the Twelve, was not with them when Jesus came. So the other disciples said to him, "We have seen the Lord." But he said to them, "Unless I see the mark of the nails in his hands and put my finger into the nail marks and put my hand into his side, I will not believe." Now a week later his disciples were again inside and Thomas was with them. Jesus came, although the doors were locked, and stood in their midst and said, "Peace be with you." Then he said to Thomas, "Put your finger here and see my hands, and bring your hand and put it into my side, and do not be unbelieving, but believe." Thomas answered and said to him, "My Lord and my God!" Jesus said to him, "Have you come to believe because you have seen me? Blessed are those who have not seen and have believed." (John 20:24–29)

Jesus, who stood before Didymus, is the same Jesus who is truly present in the Eucharistic Bread. Did you know that the name "Didymus" means "Twin"? We are never told who the twin is, but many saints have spiritually understood it to mean us Christian believers. Jesus was present to Didymus and came to him "although the doors were locked," and it is the same Jesus who comes to us behind the doors of the tabernacle and veiled bread. We are called to believe even though our eyes do not see him physically as Didymus did.

When Jesus teaches us at the Last Supper that the bread and the wine are his Body and Blood, he means it. He is not playing games with us, tricking us, or out to deceive us. He has our best interest in mind. We have to trust him. The same goes for his Real Presence at Holy Mass. He is truly there, Body, Blood, Soul, and Divinity.

Have you ever thought about why Our Lord chose to remain hidden — disguised, if you will — in the Holy Eucharist? Why not remain with us bodily or in some other manner in which our senses could behold him? He hides himself because he wants us to trust him. Trust is faith in action. Trust is what the devil lacks. The devil knows who Jesus is and where he is truly present. The devil knows that Jesus is truly present in the Blessed Sacrament, but the devil doesn't trust Jesus. The devil actually believes that God is a trickster, a liar, and a deceiver who doesn't have our best interest in mind. The trustful believer, on the other hand, knows that Jesus is present in the Eucharist. The man of great faith knows that Jesus is trustworthy and means no harm. You show your love and trust in Jesus when you believe what he has said and taught about his Real Presence.

In the Old Testament, the Jewish people believed that God was present in the Holy of Holies despite the fact that only the high priest was allowed access to the Holy of Holies once a year on the Day of Atonement. The Jews believed without seeing. Christianity is the fulfillment of Judaism and requires an even greater faith since we, too, do not see the presence of God manifested before us in physical form. Yet we know that he is truly present in the Sacred Host, the Holy of Holies.

Do you have this kind of trusting faith? If you do not, ask for it. Beg Jesus for it. He will give it to you. Ask for it for yourself and those in your family. They must come to accept the gift of faith themselves, but by cooperating with God, being humble and repenting of sin, you can help bring others to accept the gift of faith. You can help others come to believe in the Real Presence.

> The mark of the Christian is the willingness to look for the divine in the flesh of a babe in a crib, the continuing Christ under the appearance of bread on an altar.[2]
>
> — Venerable Fulton J. Sheen

Reflection Questions

1. Can you think of additional reasons why our Lord hides himself in the Holy Eucharist?
2. How do you trust Jesus?
3. If you experience doubts concerning Jesus' Real Presence, what can you do to strengthen your faith?

Resolution

Today, ask our Eucharistic Lord to increase your faith in his Real Presence. Make an unwavering act of trust and pray for your family members, friends, and coworkers who do not believe in this great mystery of love.

Prayer

Dear Jesus, my Eucharistic Lord, I praise you and adore your Real Presence in the Holy Eucharist. Forgive me for any times I have doubted your Real Presence. Jesus, I trust in you! Our Lady of the Most Blessed Sacrament, give me a share of your faith. Intercede for me that I might never abandon our Eucharistic Lord. Saint Joseph, pray for me that I may have boundless trust in Jesus Christ. Saint Peter Julian Eymard,

Apostle of the Eucharist, fill me with your Eucharistic zeal so that I might love the Blessed Sacrament above all things.

Pray the Litany of the Holy Eucharist (page 163)

DAY 12
Eucharistic Piety

Retreat Master: St. Peter Julian Eymard

Holy Communion above all must be the end [the goal] of piety. Holy Communion is the supreme act of the love of Jesus Christ for man; it is the uttermost limit of his grace, the extension of the Incarnation; it is Jesus Christ uniting himself in reality to each communicant.

Any form of piety, in order to be entirely within its grace and adapted to its end, must be Eucharistic. Brooks and rivers flow into the sea; in much the same way, everything in the Christian life leads to the ocean of this adorable Sacrament.[1]

In the Eucharist, his love outdoes itself, as it were; for this Sacrament is not only the supreme act of his love but the summary of all the acts of his love. It is even the end of all the other mysteries of his life; for Jesus died on the Cross in order to begin his Eucharistic life; or, according to St. Alphonsus Liguori, to give to his priests a sacrificial victim, and, to the faithful, the flesh of that divine victim.[2]

Reflection

Holy Communion is the supreme act of the love of Jesus Christ for man.

Any form of piety must be Eucharistic.

In the Eucharist, his love outdoes itself.

Piety is one of the Seven Gifts of the Holy Spirit. To love God and be holy — to become a saint — you must be pious. You must have Eucharistic piety. Some saints expressed their Eucharistic piety by fleeing to the desert, doing penance, and spending long hours in contemplation and thanksgiving for the gift of the Holy Eucharist. Others expressed their

Eucharistic piety in serving the sick, the poor, and the destitute in city streets. Still others expressed their Eucharistic piety by becoming missionaries, preaching in foreign lands, and catechizing thousands of people and teaching them about the Holy Eucharist. No matter what particular work, charism, or apostolate the saints were involved in, the one thing they all shared was their joy in receiving Holy Communion devoutly and piously. If you want to know a saint's secret to holiness, look no further than the Holy Eucharist.

Saints are superheroes. Superheroes have superpowers. A saint's superpower is the Holy Eucharist. You, too, are called to be a saint with a superpower. Piety toward the Eucharist is the key to having extraordinary holiness and sanctity. The Eucharist is your superpower.

Let's look at some ways of expressing Eucharistic piety.

Do you arrive early for Mass, right as it is beginning, or are you always late? What would a saint do? A saint would arrive early. Yes, there are exceptions, but what would a saint do as a norm? If you love the Eucharist, you arrive early to Holy Mass and prepare your heart. For secular events, you would never intentionally arrive at the moment a dignitary began their speech or during the third inning of a baseball game. Neither should you arrive late or at the last second for your weekly encounter with the Holy Eucharist. It is Jesus you are going to see. He is greater than all secular dignitaries or celebrities. Jesus is God.

How do you dress when you go to church? Is it the same way you dress for picnics, hikes, and walks on the beach? Again, there are always exceptions and circumstances that arise, but the exception should not be the norm. How would a saint dress for Mass? A saint would dress as well as they could, and modestly. No female saint would wear miniskirts, tight leggings, or have their breasts exposed in any way. Likewise, no male saint would wear concert shirts or drooping pants hanging down to their knees. Neither should you. You wouldn't go to see a president or a king in such a casual way, would you? Today, many have become too casual about how we dress for Holy Mass. Isn't God worthy enough that you put on nice clothes and give him your "Sunday best"?

If you are a woman, do you ever wear a beautiful dress to Holy Mass or don a lovely veil when attending Mass? Contrary to the gender confusion that plagues our times, these practices are lovely and express the beauty of the feminine. They are dignified, respectful, and modest, and men find them attractive. Again, there are always exceptions, but the exception should not be the norm. If you are a man, do you ever wear a collared shirt, slacks, and a suit jacket to Holy Mass? Women will love you for it. How you dress to attend Holy Mass says something about your belief and love for the Real Presence.

How do you genuflect to the tabernacle when you are in church? Is it hastily done? Do you make the sign of the Cross at lightning speed with no reverence or piety whatsoever? Would a saint do that? What is the harm in genuflecting slowly and deliberately, allowing your knee to rest on the floor for several seconds before standing up? Many people genuflect so poorly that they don't even realize they are facing in the wrong direction because they aren't paying attention to what they are doing. Don't do it so fast. Slow down. Be pious.

How do you receive Holy Communion? Do you receive it on the tongue or in the hand? If you receive it in the hand, why? The interior disposition of the communicant is always what matters the most, but external actions mean something and teach something. Externals manifest the interior.

Have you ever received Holy Communion on the tongue? If not, why not? For centuries, receiving Holy Communion on the tongue was the norm. It's still the norm. The Church has only permitted the reception of Holy Communion in the hand by way of an indult (an exception to the law), and only in those parts of the world where the local bishops have requested the indult from the Holy See.[3] You may be surprised to learn that the distribution of Holy Communion in the hand is not allowed in many dioceses throughout the world. What has been the fruit where the indult has been granted? It's not good. It can't be denied that belief in the Real Presence has dramatically decreased, and abuses and profanations have greatly increased, in those places where the indult has been granted. To address these concerns, the Congregation for Divine Worship and the Discipline of the Sacraments (now called the Dicastery for Divine Worship and the Discipline of the Sacraments) published a document in 2004 that deals with how the faithful are to receive Holy Communion. The document was approved by Pope John Paul II (now Pope St. John Paul II). It is titled *"Redemptionis Sacramentum*: On Certain Matters to Be Observed or to Be Avoided Regarding the Most Holy Eucharist." Below is a pertinent section:

> Although each of the faithful always has the right to receive Holy Communion on the tongue, at his choice, if any communicant should wish to receive the Sacrament in the hand, in areas where the Bishops' Conference with the *recognitio* of the Apostolic See has given permission, the sacred host is to be administered to him or her. However, special care should be taken to ensure that the host is consumed by the communicant in the presence of the minister, so that no onegoes away carrying the Eucharistic species in his hand. If there is a risk of profanation, then Holy Communion should not be given in the hand to the faithful.[4]

Did you know that receiving Holy Communion in the hand increases the risk of particles of the Sacred Host falling to the ground and being trampled on? This is a Eucharistic profanation. However, the reception of Holy Communion on the tongue greatly decreases the chance that particles of the Eucharist fall to the ground and get stepped on. Is it a sin, then, to receive Holy Communion in the hand? No, it is not a sin since the Church *permits* it. However, if you want to live a life of Eucharistic piety, why would you want to receive Holy Communion in the hand, knowing of the increased potential for small pieces of the Eucharist to fall to the ground and be stepped on? Pray about this.

Perhaps you don't receive Holy Communion on the tongue because you are too self-conscious, thinking you look foolish opening your mouth and sticking out your tongue. Okay, fair enough. However, if that is the case, practice at home in a mirror. The priest will appreciate it. A priest needs a decent amount of space on your tongue to place the consecrated Host. He doesn't need a gaping mouth, akin to a mother bird feeding her chicks. A priest also needs more than a barely opened mouth and visible tongue, as if placing a coin in a vending machine. Likewise, you should not extend your lips or teeth to take the Sacred Host from his hand because you will end up biting the Host or clamping down on it with your lips. Also, you are not to lunge your tongue out in the manner of a lizard eating prey. It can't be stressed enough that practicing at home in a mirror will resolve these issues and give you peace of mind that you are doing it correctly and reverently. Practice makes perfect.

If you are a bishop, priest, or a deacon, do you offer an example of piety at Holy Mass? Are you sloppy in your gestures, genuflections, and the way you distribute Holy Communion? People watch you. Be pious. You should have interior and exterior piety. God expects it of you. In recent times, there are bishops, priests, and deacons who refuse to give Holy Communion to people on the tongue or when they kneel. Do you refuse to administer Holy Communion on the tongue to God's people? Do you refuse to give Holy Communion to a person who is kneeling? No saintly clergy would act in such a manner. You shouldn't act this way either. Are you afraid of germs? Of death? Be a man. Be pious. Be a saint!

Reflection Questions

1. How did the saints receive Holy Communion?
2. Are there any pious practices at Holy Mass that you need to improve on?
3. How can you make the Eucharist the end (the goal) of all your piety?

Resolution

Today, examine all the forms of piety you do at Holy Mass. Strive to orient them more toward the Blessed Sacrament. Desire to live a more fervent, devout, and pious life when at Holy Mass, receiving Holy Communion, and when in the presence of the Blessed Sacrament.

Prayer

Dear Jesus, my Eucharistic Lord, thank you for always uniting yourself to me and showering me with endless graces despite my unworthiness. A thousand lifetimes would never be enough to thank you for the Holy Eucharist. Our Lady of the Most Blessed Sacrament, help me to imitate you and all the saints in being pious toward the Eucharist. Saint Joseph, help me to be pious in my heart and in my actions at Holy Mass. Saint Peter Julian Eymard, Apostle of the Eucharist, fill me with your Eucharistic zeal so that I might love the Blessed Sacrament above all things.

Pray the Litany of the Most Precious Blood (page 166)

DAY 13
Recollection

Retreat Master: St. Peter Julian Eymard

We who wish to live with the Eucharist must, more than anyone else, live an interior life. In the Eucharist the life of Jesus Christ is all interior. He conceals his body so that we may go to his mind and heart. He speaks to the soul only.

But to reach this state of interior life, there is one road only, that of recollection. This is an unquestionable truth little known or appreciated even by pious people. It is certain that a grace of recollection draws us closer to God and obtains for us more light and fervor, because we are then, so to speak, nearer to the fire.[1]

Charity, the virtues, and external works are, and must be, only branches; the same is true for vocal prayer. The life of these works lies entirely in recollection, in the union of the soul in God. It is its nourishment, its life and strength. That is why you must come closer to God in prayer, listen to him, rather than always speak to him, be recollected in homage at his feet rather than perform acts of generosity where the soul ordinarily puts aside its recollection to become scattered by sentiments that are foreign to it. The activity of the soul is often our great enemy.[2]

If you need to economize your time, let it be for greater recollection and union with God.[3]

Reflection

We must live an interior life.

In the Eucharist the life of Jesus Christ is all interior.

Be recollected at his feet rather than perform acts of generosity where the soul ordinarily puts aside its recollection to become scattered.

Many Catholics are too busy. Doing this, doing that. Going here, going there. It's not that their intentions are bad, but often times the result of constant activity is that people are not recollected. People can mistakenly think that activity means spiritual depth. This is not necessarily the case. Remember what Jesus told Martha: "Martha, Martha, you are anxious and worried about many things; only one thing is necessary" (Luke 10:41–42). That one necessary thing is spending time at the feet of Jesus in prayer and recollection.

What is recollection and how do we practice it? Our Retreat Master explains it this way: "To recollect oneself, as the word itself implies, means to gather, to draw oneself from the outside to the inside."[4] He also states, "The door which introduces us into the dwelling of Jesus — is holy recollection."[5] To be recollected means to live an interior life, always aware that you are in the presence of God. The person who is recollected is interiorly still, tranquil, and attentive to God speaking in the depths of their heart, mind, and soul. People who are recollected know that their dignity and worth do not come from constant activity, but from who they are in relation to God's love. Recollected people are prayerful people.

This understanding of recollection explains how someone like St. Teresa of Calcutta, an extremely busy missionary, was also able to be an extremely recollected woman. Her life shows us that recollection and activity are not mutually exclusive, but the priority is always prayer and silence before God. Thus, her life reveals that it is only the person who maintains an interior and consistent prayer life who can be recollected while in the midst of activities. The recollected can be busy, but the busy can't be recollected unless they are prayerful.

Many Catholics today have been taught that "active participation" at Holy Mass means that you have to be doing something other than simply being present in the pew and worshiping God in silence. This is not true. You are not worshiping God any less by having no other role at Holy Mass than being in the pew. In fact, you will most likely be the most recollected at Mass because you are free of tasks and can enter deeply into the Holy Sacrifice of the Mass, while those who are doing things are more likely to be distracted and unable to maintain recollection. Read again one of the statements made by our Retreat Master at the beginning of today's readings: "You must come closer to God in prayer, listen to him, rather than always speak to him, be recollected in homage at his feet rather than perform acts of generosity where the soul ordinarily puts aside its recollection to become scattered by sentiments that are foreign to it. The activity of the soul is often our great enemy." Recollection is possible in the midst of busy activity, of course, but it takes a very holy person to balance both. It takes a holy priest to maintain recollection and activity at Mass as well.

Active participation in Holy Mass does not mean you must have a ministerial function. You don't need to be a lector, in the choir, an altar boy, or have any other role than being a participant in the pew. These days, many people want a "Participation Award" or a trophy for attendance or any participation whatsoever. Believe it or not, the priest can do all the functions at Mass. He can sing, read, serve, and administer Holy Communion all by himself. It's his job.

In recent times, a particular ministry has become ubiquitous and commonplace in many parishes and dioceses, namely, the Extraordinary Minister of Holy Communion. In some instances, it can be a needed function and helpful in particular situations. Nonetheless, how did something intended to be "extraordinary" become "ordinary"? After all, the correct title for this function is "Extraordinary Minister of Holy Communion" (EMHC) not "Eucharistic Minister" (EM). There is no such function or title of "Eucharistic Minister."

Now, to be clear, it is not a sin to be an Extraordinary Minister of Holy Communion. The Church permits it in extraordinary situations. However, taking on such a function should only be done if it is absolutely necessary. There must be a true discerned need for such a role. If trained well,

Extraordinary Ministers of Holy Communion can bring Holy Communion to the sick in hospitals and nursing homes, as well as to the homebound who are unable to attend church due to illness, disability, or old age. People who serve as Extraordinary Ministers of Holy Communion can be helpful if a large parish only has one priest or if a priest is aged or has a disability of some kind. However, that being said, it is still not the norm. Priests and deacons are the ordinary ministers of Holy Communion. This isn't clericalism, either. It's normal liturgical protocol and procedure. Men are ordained priests and deacons in order to dedicate their lives to the Eucharist and its distribution. Priests and deacons have a job to do. The lay faithful should not usurp their role. Neither should priests and deacons avoid their duties and give their responsibilities to the laity.

On occasion, the use of Extraordinary Ministers of Holy Communion at Mass is justifiable if Holy Mass will be unduly prolonged. For example, if there is only one priest distributing Holy Communion to a thousand people or more, it might necessitate the assistance of an Extraordinary Minister of Holy Communion. This is an extreme example, of course. In most instances, what's the rush? If it takes a little longer to distribute Holy Communion because there is only one ordained minister, what's the big deal? Are people incapable of spending a little more time in church with Jesus inside them while the ordained minister does his job and gives Holy Communion to others? After receiving Holy Communion, isn't having more time for personal prayer a good thing? Wouldn't it help foster a Eucharistic revival and a Eucharistic people? Wouldn't it help foster prayer and recollection? Sure it would. Bonus: arriving at church early means you can get the front seats, which will give you more recollected prayer time with Jesus as the priest distributes the Eucharist to those in the back. Worrying about how long the distribution of Holy Communion takes is a modern issue. It wasn't an issue when parishes had altar rails. The method of distributing Holy Communion using an altar rail is extremely efficient and inherently reverent. It's how it was done for centuries, and it worked. All ordinary ministers of Holy Communion (ordained men) and members of the laity who serve as Extraordinary Ministers of Holy Communion should read the official documents of the Church regarding the distribution of Holy Communion.[6] Becoming familiar with these documents is a great way to ensure that things are being done properly and that abuses are not taking place.

If you are an Extraordinary Minister of Holy Communion, are you certain you are doing it as it was intended to be done? When you bring Holy Communion to people in hospitals, nursing homes, and other places, do you ever mention, at least on occasion, that Confession to a priest is needed first for anyone who is in mortal sin? This needs to be done lovingly and in the right context, of course, but it does need to be done. Do you presume that because you are an Extraordinary Minister of Holy Communion that you can open the tabernacle at will and take Sacred Hosts? Do you properly clean the pyx and other sacred vessels used for such a noble ministry? Do you find yourself more recollected at Mass in your role as an Extraordinary Minister of Holy Communion, or are you less recollected? Remember: God doesn't love you any less if you are not an Extraordinary Minister of Holy Communion. The Virgin Mary was not an Extraordinary Minister of Holy Communion. Your dignity comes from being a child of God. Pray about these things.

If you are a bishop, a priest, or a deacon, are you allowing something that was intended to be extraordinary to be ordinary? Whether the lay faithful become Extraordinary Ministers of Holy Communion is your decision. They don't appoint themselves. Such a function requires your affirmation and approval. Are you too readily giving permission for this ministry? Are you helping souls be recollected at Mass or unnecessarily giving them your duties, duties that take them away from recollection? As our Retreat Master notes,

"Recollection is the beginning of paradise. But as no one enters heaven except after having suffered, so it is with recollection, since it is defined as life in God, with God."[7] Brothers, if you suffer for the greater good, which might require you to spend a few additional minutes distributing Holy Communion, you will bear much fruit and have many holy spiritual children. Your parish and diocese can experience a Eucharistic revival by your pious leadership and loving decisions and actions. Your parishioners can grow in Eucharistic recollection under your watchful and loving care. Pray about these things.

Reflection Questions
1. Are you recollected when at Holy Mass and in your daily activities?
2. What are some practical ways you can grow in recollection?
3. How can your interior recollection impact your participation at Holy Mass?

Resolution
Today, close your eyes and think about our Eucharistic Lord in the tabernacle. Offer him your love, devotion, and adoration. Know that his Eucharistic heart beats for you. Ask for the grace to be more recollected and willing to separate yourself from anything in your life that takes away your Eucharistic recollection.

Prayer
Dear Jesus, my Eucharistic Lord, help me to always be aware of your Real Presence. Grant me the grace to live a recollected Eucharistic life from this day forward. Detach my heart from the things of this world and help me to have boundless trust in Divine Providence. Our Lady of the Most Blessed Sacrament, model of recollection, guide me to be Eucharistic in my recollection, even in the midst of my daily responsibilities. Saint Joseph, master of the interior life, teach me quietness of

soul and stillness of heart. Saint Peter Julian Eymard, Apostle of the Eucharist, fill me with your Eucharistic zeal so that I might love the Blessed Sacrament above all things.

Pray the Litany of the Holy Eucharist (page 163)

DAY 14
Reverence and Silence

Retreat Master: St. Peter Julian Eymard

Watch a saint enter a church. He goes in without concerning himself with those who are already there.

Remain quiet for a moment after you have come into church; silence is the greatest mark of respect, and the first disposition of prayer is respect.[1]

Holy Church expects profound reverence before the Blessed Sacrament, especially when it is exposed. Silence must then be still more absolute, one's behavior still more respectful; the restraint of keeping recollected is already by itself a beautiful homage of virtue.

During exposition, holy liturgy rules out the simple genuflection and prescribes the prostration of two knees, in imitation of the twenty-four ancients before the throne of the Lamb in heaven.[2]

Protect your moments of silence and solitude: the soul needs them and God wants them to visit souls and converse with the heart which dwells in his love.[3] Go often to rest in silence before the divine tabernacle. That is how you will renew your strength and rediscover your courage.[4]

Reflection

Remain quiet for a moment after you have come into church.

Silence is the greatest mark of respect.

Protect your moments of silence and solitude.

What would it be like to see your favorite saint praying before the Blessed Sacrament? It would probably move you to tears. A saint's devotion, reverence, and silence before the Real Presence would leave no doubt in your mind that Jesus is truly present in the Holy Eucharist.

Shouldn't this be the case with all Catholics? Shouldn't this be the case with all clergy? What about you? Are you reverent in church? Are you quiet in church? Would someone who saw you praying before the Blessed Sacrament be inspired by your example of Eucharistic piety?

If you are doing these things, praise God! Many are not observing these things in church. Too many people arrive late for Holy Mass and leave immediately after Holy Communion so as to get out of the parking lot before everybody else. Before Holy Mass in many parishes, people are conversing in and over the pews, the choir is rehearsing, and those involved with various functions at Mass are running around doing last-minute tasks. Some of these things are unavoidable, of course, but it does seem that silence before and after Mass is rare these days. With so much noise, are people truly able to prepare their hearts for the celebration of Holy Mass? Are they able to give thanks and pray in silence after Mass? In many parishes, people would find a peaceful and quiet preparation and thanksgiving very hard to do.

Sometimes the priest himself is busy as a beaver before Holy Mass, offering very little witness to recollection and prayer. Priests don't need to be stoic in a corner praying, of course, but your average person in a parish rarely sees their priest at prayer before, after, or outside of Holy Mass. When is the last time you saw your priest on his knees before a tabernacle praying? Have you ever seen him pray before or after Holy Mass? Most people have never seen this from their priest. What would happen if people came to church and saw their pastor kneeling before the tabernacle in prayer preparing for Holy Mass? Silence. That is what would happen. That silence would change everything. People coming inside would stop talking and imitate the priest, their father, kneeling down to pray and recollect themselves in preparation for Holy Mass. Do not all children imitate their parents?

What about after Mass? What would happen if instead of going outside the church to shake hands with everyone and wish them a great day, the priest returned to the sanctuary, knelt down, and prayed in thanksgiving for the Eucharist? He doesn't have to make a grand display about it, but his actions would undoubtedly spark a Eucharistic revival in that parish. No useless committee work needed. No strategic planning required. No funds spent.

One of the problems today in many parishes is that people are uncomfortable with silence and think they have to be constantly listening to something or someone. Many parishes and shrines these days even have nonstop music playing from speakers during the week when people just want to step inside, away from the noise, and say some prayers. Are we that uncomfortable with silence that we have to turn our churches into music studios? It's not that the relaxing music or chant playing in the background is bad or evil. But silence is a good thing, and we should have more of it in our churches.

Reflection Questions

1. How can you show more reverence during Holy Mass?
2. Why is silence so important for your prayer life?
3. What are some ways you can incorporate more silence into your life?

Resolution

Today, make a decision that the next time you attend Holy Mass, you will enter and leave the church in an attitude and atmosphere of reverence and silence. Once Holy Mass ends, remain in church and pray in thanksgiving for receiving Jesus.

Prayer

Dear Jesus, my Eucharistic Lord, I love you with all my heart. Forgive me for the times when I have not been reverent or silent in your presence. Forgive me also for the times when I have simply gone through the motions while my heart was far from you. Our Lady of the Most Blessed Sacrament, help me to imitate your reverence and silence before Jesus' holy presence. Saint Joseph, reverent and silent man, teach me to be like you. Saint Peter Julian Eymard, Apostle of the Eucharist, fill me with your Eucharistic zeal so that I might love the Blessed Sacrament above all things.

Pray the Litany of the Most Precious Blood (page 166)

DAY 15
Eucharistic Adoration

Retreat Master: St. Peter Julian Eymard

The object of Eucharistic adoration is the divine Person of our Lord Jesus Christ, present in the Blessed Sacrament. There is nothing greater or holier we can do on earth than this adoration. Eucharistic adoration is the greatest of actions. To adore is to share the life of Mary on earth when she adored the Word Incarnate in her virginal womb, when she adored him in the crib, on Calvary, and in the Divine Eucharist.[1]

Adoration is a dialogue. It is made at the feet of our Lord living and present. The adorer must speak to him, question him, listen, and respond.

Merely to read without giving the heart time to pour itself out in sweet converse with our Lord, would be to deprive this good Master of what he looks for in our visits. Jesus is a prisoner, he expects from us some words of comfort. He is our friend, and he loves to hear us express our affection.

We should, then, close our book from time to time, making use of it only as a guide, an outline, and speak with our heart as best we know. Our Lord understands all dialects, and he pays little attention to the purity of language if it comes from a loving heart.[2]

The adorer should not leave the presence of the Divine Master without thanking him for his audience of love, ask his forgiveness for distractions and lack of reverence, offer him as a sign of fidelity a flower of virtue, a bouquet of little sacrifices, then leave the place as from the Cenacle, like an angel leaving the throne of God to go and carry out his divine orders.[3]

Reflection

There is nothing greater or holier we can do on earth than adoration.

Eucharistic adoration is the greatest of actions.

Our Eucharistic Lord is our friend, and he loves to hear us express our affection.

When our Retreat Master says there is nothing greater we can do on earth than adoration, he is not saying that Eucharistic adoration is greater than the Holy Sacrifice of the Mass and receiving Holy Communion. What he presumes every Catholic knows is that we not only adore Jesus in the Blessed Sacrament outside of Mass, but also during Mass and when we have received Holy Communion. This has always been the teaching of the Church, and it always will be the teaching of the Church. How strange it is, then, that there are priests and even bishops who say that we do not adore Jesus in the Blessed Sacrament at Holy Mass. They posit that the Mass is not about adoration of the Real Presence but about the community present. Certainly, community is important and needed, but God always comes first. If you don't get the order correct, you end up with a very distorted understanding of just about everything.

We are called to receive Jesus in the Holy Eucharist at Holy Mass *and* adore him in the Blessed Sacrament at Holy Mass. The priest says as much when he elevates the Sacred Host and proclaims, "Behold the Lamb of God! Behold him who takes away the sins of the world!" At that moment, we are to gaze upon our Eucharistic Lord in adoration and awe. We adore the Eucharist again when the priest stands before us, elevates the Sacred Host, and says to each of us before the reception of Holy Communion, "The Body of Christ." The response from our lips is "Amen," while our eyes and heart adore the gaze at the Eucharist in adoration. Then, once we have received Holy Communion, we adore him truly present inside us. God's holiness and justice demand that we adore him at Holy Mass.

We also have the privilege of adoring the Blessed Sacrament outside of Mass. Eucharistic exposition and adoration is a tremendous gift to God's people. Its fruits bless both the individual and the world. Eucharistic adoration is a special time of intimacy between a soul and God. Whether at Mass or outside of Mass, adoration of the Blessed Sacrament is the greatest thing we can do![4]

Have you ever gone to Eucharistic adoration? It's not hard to do. The first step requires finding out where the nearest parish or shrine is located in your diocese that offers Eucharistic adoration. Some parishes or shrines have adoration chapels and expose the Blessed Sacrament perpetually or have adoration on certain days of the week. Why not pray about signing up for an hour a week? It will transform your life. You will find yourself falling more in love with Jesus, having more peace in your life, and not stressing out over all the chaos that life throws at you.

Sitting in silence before the Blessed Sacrament reading the Bible or the lives of the saints, praying a rosary, or just gazing upon the miracle of the Holy Eucharist is never pointless or a waste of time. Eucharistic adoration is always spiritually fruitful. It unites you with God, gives peace, and makes the world a better place. You can enter an adoration chapel with a thousand worries, concerns, and problems, but after spending time with the Blessed Sacrament you can leave with an inner tranquility that the world can't take away. There really is nothing like it. The presence of Jesus blesses you, every single time. Your problems and hardships in life will be waiting for you when you leave, but *you* will be different. Adoration changes *you*. In life, there are many things that can't be changed. People get sick, loved ones die, tragedy happens. But when you spend time with Jesus in adoration, it is you who change because you have opened yourself up to the transforming power of his love.

If there is no parish or shrine in your area that offers exposition of the Blessed Sacrament, don't let that be the reason you don't go and visit Jesus at all. While it is truly wonderful to gaze upon the Sacred Host with your eyes and adore him, Jesus is just as present to you when the doors of the tabernacle are closed as when he is exposed in a monstrance. Adoration requires faith, not sight. Don't miss the grace of spending time with Jesus and adoring him, whether exposed for you to see or behind the tabernacle doors. Your time here on earth is but the blink of an eye compared to eternity.

Let us make frequent and devout visits to God in the tabernacle.[5]

— Blessed James Alberione

Have a great devotion to the Holy Sacrament; don't miss the opportunities to visit, adore, and love him.[6]

— St. Paul of the Cross

Like St. John, all are called to become beloved disciples. All we need is to become Eucharistic souls, adoring souls, allowing God to work those wonders in us, which only he can do.[7]

— Blessed Carlo Acutis

Reflection Questions

1. Why is Eucharistic adoration the greatest action you can do in this life?
2. What areas in your life take precedence over the Holy Eucharist?
3. How can you improve your Eucharistic adoration?

Resolution

Today, take the time to find out where there is Eucharistic adoration in your area. Plan to make a visit before the end of this Eucharistic retreat. If there is a Perpetual Adoration chapel in your area, pray about signing up for an hour a week. Your life will never be the same!

Prayer

Dear Jesus, my Eucharistic Lord, I believe you are truly present Body, Blood, Soul, and Divinity in the Sacred Host. I long to adore you at Holy Mass, exposed in a monstrance, and behind the tabernacle doors. I kneel before you in profound gratitude and humility for the gift of the Blessed Sacrament. Our Lady of the Blessed Sacrament, help me to adore your Eucharistic Son. Give me your eyes, your faith, your humility, and most of all your love for Jesus. Saint Joseph, teach me to delight in adoring Jesus at Holy Mass and outside of Holy Mass. Saint Peter Julian Eymard, Apostle of the Eucharist, fill me with your Eucharistic zeal so that I might love the Blessed Sacrament above all things.

Pray the Litany of the Holy Eucharist (page 163)

DAY 16
The Sacred Heart

Retreat Master: St. Peter Julian Eymard

This divine heart is living and palpitating in the Eucharist, no longer of a passible and mortal life, open to sadness, agony, and pain, but of a life risen and consummated in blessedness.[1]

Saint Margaret Mary Alacoque received the revelation of the Sacred Heart before the Blessed Sacrament exposed. Jesus manifested himself to her in the Host, holding his heart in his hands and saying to her the adorable words, the most eloquent commentary on his presence in the Blessed Sacrament: "Behold this heart which has so loved men!"

And our Lord, appearing to Mother Mechtilde, foundress of a society of women-adorers, commanded her to love ardently and honor his Sacred Heart in the Blessed Sacrament as much as she could; and he gave it to her as a pledge of his love, to be her refuge in life and consolation at the hour of death.[2]

Adore the deep wound in the Sacred Heart of Jesus; place yourself below this divine wound, so that the water flowing from it may purify you, and its divine blood sanctify you. Kiss this divine wound, breathe in the beautiful and lively flame which issues from it. Enter into this divine dwelling, place your heart there, in union with his.[3]

Plunge yourself more deeply into this source of grace and love. It is the grace of our time, since our Lord is giving us his heart to be adored, loved and glorified, because he is complaining about indifference and ingratitude.[4]

Reflection

The Sacred Heart is living and palpitating in the Eucharist.
Adore the deep wound in the Sacred Heart of Jesus.
Our Lord is giving us his heart to be adored.

Have you heard about Eucharistic miracles? They are extraordinary and rare events that have taken place over the centuries, attesting to the truth that the Sacred Host is indeed flesh and blood. The miracles generally involve a Sacred Host oozing blood or a portion of the Eucharist becoming visible as flesh. In many instances, God brought about the Eucharistic miracle when a person involved in the occult obtained a consecrated Host with the intention of profaning it, desecrating it, or committing an act of sacrilege against it. Something that makes these miracles even more incredible is that they are still preserved and visible for people to see, even though many of them date back centuries.

The well-known eighth-century Eucharistic miracle in Lanciano, Italy, confirms that the heart of Jesus is present in the Blessed Sacrament. Scientific studies done on the Eucharistic miracle of Lanciano have discovered that the visible flesh in the Sacred Host is heart tissue. In the case of the more recent Eucharistic miracle out of Buenos Aires, Argentina, the heart tissue shows signs of having undergone tremendous stress, the kind of stress that an organ undergoes when something violent and traumatic has occurred. Interestingly, when our Lord revealed his Sacred Heart to St. Margaret Mary Alacoque it was surrounded by thorns. Jesus said the following to this great saint:

> Behold this heart which has so loved men, and has spared nothing, even to consuming itself, in order to show them its love; and in return, I receive nothing but ingratitude from the greater number through the contempt, the irreverence, the sacrileges, and the coldness shown towards me in this Sacrament of Love. But, what is more painful to

me, is that these are hearts which are consecrated to me.[5]

Although Jesus is in heaven with his Father and the Holy Spirit, in some mysterious way our sins still wound him, especially his heart in the Holy Eucharist. The revelations given to St. Margaret Mary Alacoque teach us that the Holy Eucharist is a person, a divine person, with a divine heart. The Eucharistic heart of Jesus beats for us because it is the Sacred Heart of Jesus.

> The Eucharist is truly the heart of Jesus.[6]
>
> — Blessed Carlo Acutis

> Devotion to Christ's heart cannot be separated from the Eucharist, the sacrament of the Lord's Body and Blood.[7] All devotion to the heart of Jesus and all its manifestations are profoundly Eucharistic.[8]
>
> — Pope St. John Paul II

When we adore our Lord in the Holy Eucharist, and receive him in Holy Communion in a state of grace, we console his Sacred Heart and comfort his heart that loves us so much. We console and comfort his Eucharistic heart because every time the Eucharist is desecrated, blasphemed, or received unworthily, the Sacred Heart of Jesus in the Eucharist is pained and offended by the lack of love shown to his divine person. For this reason many saints have sought to make reparation to the Eucharistic heart of Jesus in the Eucharist.

> Fly in spirit to Jesus' Eucharistic heart, and there be consumed with sorrow for the disrespect he gets from bad Christians.[9]
>
> — St. Paul of the Cross

O heart of Jesus, heart outraged by incredulity, by forgetfulness, and by the contradictions of mankind, have pity still on your heritage, and do not abandon it to the fury of your enemies. We know well that not all these enemies are those who do not know you or who deny your presence among us; some of them even partake of your sacred banquet with cold and indifferent souls or even with souls infected by the hideous leprosy of sin, thus wounding your heart most dolorously even in the house of those who love you.[10]

— Blessed Basil Moreau

Our Lord asked me to console his heart desecrated in the Holy Eucharist.[11]

— Blessed Dina Bélanger

I will comfort the most sweet Eucharistic heart continuously and will play harmonious melodies on the strings of my heart.[12]

— St. Faustina Kowalska

The Sacred Heart of Jesus in the Eucharist wants to be loved. Before the tabernacle, you can console Jesus and make amends for the many sins that wound his heart. Before the tabernacle, you can apply the balm of love to his pierced and wounded heart. The Eucharistic heart of Jesus is waiting for you!

This heart is our refuge, in which the abandoned finds a home, the one asking is heard, the tempted is strengthened, the distressed receives consolation, the sinner obtains the grace of remorse and forgiveness. Therefore, in all your spiritual and earthly needs, run to this heart. And you do not need to look far for this heart, because it is alive and always beating in the Most Holy Sacrament of the Altar.[13]

— St. Joseph Sebastian Pelczar

Reflection Questions

1. Do you want to be closer to the Eucharistic Heart of Jesus?
2. How can you foster a greater devotion to the Sacred Heart present in the Holy Eucharist?
3. What are some things you can do to console the Eucharistic Heart of Jesus?

Resolution

Today, repeat the following prayer in reparation to the Eucharistic Heart of Jesus: "Most Sacred Heart of Jesus, present in the Holy Eucharist, have mercy on me. Forgive me for any times that I have pained your heart by my sins or by receiving you unworthily. Most Sacred Heart of Jesus, present in the Holy Eucharist, help me to love you above all things."

Prayer

Dear Jesus, my Eucharistic Lord, I give my heart entirely to you. Help me to love your Sacred Heart in the Most Blessed Sacrament. Our Lady of the Most Blessed Sacrament, draw me deeper into the Sacred Heart of Jesus. Saint Joseph, greatest consoler of the hearts of Jesus and Mary, I want to be more like you. Saint Peter Julian Eymard, Apostle of the Eucharist, fill me with your Eucharistic zeal so that I might love the Blessed Sacrament above all things.

Pray the Litany of the Most Precious Blood (page 166)

DAY 17
The Holy Spirit

Retreat Master: St. Peter Julian Eymard

I insist on this point: The Holy Spirit himself guides the pure and recollected soul. He is the Master, the Director.[1]

Each soul receives dispositions sympathetic to their vocation. To Eucharistic souls the Holy Spirit is, above all, the teacher of adoration in spirit and truth. It is he that gave the apostles the power and spirit of prayer.[2]

Let us learn to prepare ourselves for Communion in union with the Holy Spirit.[3]

The Holy Spirit establishes unity of sentiment in our souls so that when Jesus ceases to be with us sacramentally, he will still live in us spiritually. In this way the Holy Spirit prolongs our Communion, continuing in us the divine life of Jesus.[4]

Thank the Holy Spirit for continuing to incarnate him (Jesus) every day on the altar by the words of the priest, as he did the first time in the virginal womb of Mary.[5]

Reflection

The Holy Spirit is the teacher of adoration.

The Holy Spirit prolongs our Communion.

Thank the Holy Spirit!

The Third Person of the Holy Trinity is often overlooked and forgotten, especially in our prayer life. The majority of Christians address prayers to Jesus or God the Father. Without the Holy Spirit, however, we would not have the Eucharist. Without the Holy Spirit, we would not be able to receive and adore the Eucharistic Lord. The Holy Spirit is absolutely necessary in our spiritual lives because it is he who prays in us and helps us to receive the Blessed Sacrament worthily.

How is your relationship with the Holy Spirit? Do you have a relationship with the Holy Spirit or is it nonexistent? Do you ever pray to the Holy Spirit? Do you invite the Holy Spirit into your life and ask him to make all your actions pleasing to heaven and spiritually fruitful?

At baptism, you became a temple of the Holy Spirit. How sad that after baptism and Confirmation so many Christians have little to do with the Holy Spirit and never ask him for guidance, protection, wisdom, and growth in virtue. The Holy Spirit wants to help us. He wants to cleanse the temple of our souls of anything that is not holy. We need more of the Holy Spirit in our lives. A greater devotion to the Holy Spirit will bring about a greater devotion to the Blessed Sacrament.

Where the Blessed Sacrament is present, the Holy Spirit is present. God is a communion of love, a communion of divine persons. Each divine person shares the same divine nature. Where one is present, all are present. Every time you attend Mass or visit the Blessed Sacrament you are coming into the presence of the Holy Spirit. Although God the Father and God the Holy Spirit did not become incarnate like the Second Person of the Holy Trinity did, all three persons of the Blessed Trinity are spiritually present wherever the Blessed Sacrament is present.

Sometimes Catholics are under the impression that having a relationship with the Holy Spirit means you have to be involved in the charismatic renewal. This is not true. The Holy Spirit is for all Christians, and praying in tongues or being involved in the charismatic movement is not a requirement. What matters most is love and the Seven Gifts of the Holy Spirit (Wisdom, Understanding, Counsel, Fortitude, Knowledge, Piety, and Fear of the Lord). Otherwise, as St. Paul says, a person is just a clanging cymbal (see 1 Cor. 13:1).

To the surprise of some, the Holy Spirit is neither a dove nor a holy bird. The Bible employs such imagery to describe the divine person of the Holy Spirit since he did not become incarnate. The Holy Spirit is spirit, not flesh and blood, or an animal of some kind. The Holy Spirit does not have a body. We are able to observe, however, the effects of the Holy Spirit. The greatest effect of the Holy Spirit is observed in the Eucharist. Without the Holy Spirit, we would not have the Eucharist. When Jesus instituted the Holy Eucharist, he prayed in, with, and through the Holy Spirit to bring it about. This is why at every Holy Mass, the priest says the "Epiclesis" (invocation of the Holy Spirit) over the bread and wine. This action calls down the Holy Spirit so that the bread and wine become (are transubstantiated into) the Body and Blood of Jesus Christ. It's why bells were traditionally rung at this solemn moment of Mass. It's the moment when the Holy Spirit is acting in a powerful way.

The Holy Spirit doesn't leave when the priest is done praying the Epiclesis. Once the bread and wine are transformed (transubstantiated) into the Body and Blood of Jesus, the Holy Spirit remains, both for the duration of Mass as well as wherever the Eucharistic Jesus is located (that is, inside your body and soul, or inside the tabernacle). This means that every time you receive Holy Communion, the Holy Spirit enters into your body and your soul in a most profound way. Taking it one step further, every time you visit our Eucharistic Lord reserved in the tabernacle or exposed in Eucharistic adoration, you are also encountering the Holy Spirit who is present in a unique way. These are profound mysteries.

So, the next time you attend Holy Mass or visit the Blessed Sacrament, realize that you are also encountering the Holy Spirit. Delight in him. Talk to him as you would a friend. Share your heart, mind, desires, struggles, joy, and hopes with the Holy Spirit. Ask the Holy Spirit to direct your soul and help you fall more in love with the Eucharist.

> When you become totally consumed by this Eucharistic Fire, then you will be able to thank with greater awareness the Lord God who has called you to be part of his flock and you will enjoy

that peace which those who are happy according to the world have never tasted. Because true happiness does not consist in the pleasures of the world and in earthly things, but in peace of conscience which we can have only if we are pure in heart and in mind.[6]

— Blessed Pier Giorgio Frassati

Reflection Questions

1. How can you be more receptive to the Holy Spirit?
2. How does the Holy Spirit bring you closer to the Blessed Sacrament?
3. Are you living as a temple of the Holy Spirit in your thoughts, words, and actions?

Resolution

Today, invite the Holy Spirit into your life. Implore the Holy Spirit to help you receive Holy Communion in a more pious and intentional manner. Make it a point to acknowledge the Holy Spirit at the next Holy Mass you attend.

Prayer

Dear Jesus, my Eucharistic Lord, bring me closer to the Holy Spirit, the spirit that transforms bread and wine into your Body and Blood. Holy Spirit, come into my heart and transform me so that everything I do is pleasing to the Most Holy Trinity. Our Lady, Spouse of the Holy Spirit, help me live a Holy Spirit–filled life. Saint Joseph, Vicar of the Holy Spirit, pray that I might be docile and receptive to all the movements and inspirations of the Holy Spirit. Saint Peter Julian Eymard, Apostle of the Eucharist, fill me with your Eucharistic zeal so that I might love the Blessed Sacrament above all things.

Pray the Litany of the Holy Eucharist (page 163)

DAY 18
Mary's Eucharistic Life

Retreat Master: St. Peter Julian Eymard

Jesus leads a hidden life in the Most Blessed Sacrament. He honors therein silence and solitude, these two essential conditions of life in God. He is dead to the world, to its glory, to its possessions, to its pleasures; his is a risen and heavenly life.

Such was the life of Mary after the Ascension of her divine Son. She retired to the Cenacle, on Mount Sion, and she wrapped herself up in obscurity and oblivion. The Evangelists will no longer record her wonderful sayings; neither will they report for our edification her actions so sacred, or her virtues so flawless; they have left her in the Cenacle, at the foot of the adorable Eucharist in the habitual exercise of a humble and self-effacing adoration.

Living in this center of love, she was henceforth dead to the world with her divine Son. The Divine Host was her only possession, her only glory, her only joy. Was not the Eucharist her Jesus in his entirety?[1]

Mary's contemplation before the Eucharist was of a nature that no words are adequate to describe. Jesus Christ alone, who was its object, knew its value. Mary had the most complete knowledge of the love that Jesus had shown in instituting the Eucharist. She knew what sufferings his heart had to sustain, the sacrifices exacted of him by the institution of this Sacrament: sufferings of his love against the incredulity and the indifference of the greater part of mankind; sufferings of his sanctity against impiety, the blasphemy and the sacrileges of which his Sacrament would be the object, not only on the part of heretics, but even on the part of his friends; sufferings of his goodness against the ingratitude of

Christians who neglect to receive him in Holy Commu-nion, refusing thereby his richest graces, his most tender invitation.

Mary had followed these sufferings, she had shared these sacrifices whose triumph she now witnesses; and she lives them over again in her adoration.[2]

Mary devoted herself exclusively to the Eucharistic glory of Jesus. She knew that it was the desire of the Eternal Father to make the Eucharist known, loved, and served by all men; that the need of Jesus' heart was to communicate to all men his gifts of grace and glory. She knew, too, that it was the mission of the Holy Spirit to extend and perfect in the hearts of men the reign of Jesus Christ, and that the Church had been founded only to give Jesus to the world. All Mary's desire, then, was to make him known in his Sacrament.[3]

Ever since Calvary, all men were her children. She loved them with a mother's tenderness and longed for their supreme good as for her own; therefore, she was consumed with the desire to make Jesus in the Blessed Sacrament known to all, to inflame all hearts with his love, to see them enchained to his loving service. To obtain this favor, Mary passed her time at the foot of the Most Adorable Sacrament, in prayer and penance. In her boundless zeal, she embraced the needs of the faithful everywhere, for all time to come, who would inherit the Holy Eucharist and be its adorers.[4]

Reflection

Was not the Eucharist her Jesus in his entirety?

Mary passed her time at the foot of the Most Adorable Sacrament.

She was consumed with the desire to make Jesus in the Blessed Sacrament known to all.

Mary's womb was as a living tabernacle of the Real

Presence. Within her immaculate body, just below her Immaculate Heart, the Body of Jesus grew and the Blood of Jesus flowed. Without Mary, we would not have the Eucharist. She gave flesh and blood to God!

After the Ascension of Jesus into heaven, Mary lived an entirely Eucharistic life. She attended the Holy Sacrifice of the Mass celebrated by Sts. Peter, John, Andrew, and the rest of the apostles. Can you imagine what that must have been like? Mary is the Mother of God, an immaculate creature, and closer to God than anyone ever will be, and yet she received Holy Communion from the priests just as all Christians do. She is greater in dignity and merit than every priest, bishop, or pope, but she submitted to their leadership and guidance because she knows that they represent her Divine Son. It was only through the hands of a priest that Mary received her son in Holy Communion.

Mary was not a priest. She did not desire to be a priest. Mary was not a deacon. She did not desire to be a deacon. Women are not called to ordained ministry. Why? To the modern world this seems like an injustice. The reason women are not called to be priests and deacons is because it's not how God established the order of things in the New Covenant family. Not ordaining women to the priesthood or the diaconate does not mean that men are better than women. Men and women are equal in dignity before God, but their functions and roles are different. It is not up to us to change nature and Divine Revelation. If we resist nature and Divine Revelation or rebel against them, it isn't a hierarchical Church being fought against, but God that one is fighting against.

After Jesus walked this earth, the Virgin Mary remained completely docile to the Holy Spirit, spending her days with her Eucharistic Son in Holy Communion, adoring him, and making his Real Presence known and loved. In her maternal zeal in wanting to make Jesus in the Blessed Sacrament known to the ends of the earth, she bilocated to St. James the Apostle in Spain as he sought to bring Christianity and the

Real Presence of her Son to the farthest reaches of the known world at that time. According to our Retreat Master, "The mission dearest to Mary's heart was that of constant prayer for the success of the preaching and the missionary labors of the apostles and of all the members of Jesus Christ's priesthood."[5] She, who was overshadowed by the Holy Spirit at the Annunciation, and filled with the same Spirit at Pentecost, wanted to remain overshadowed by the Spirit of God forever and promote Jesus. She did this to her last breath, and continues this maternal mission in heaven until time runs out.

Mary loved the Holy Eucharist more than anything or anyone. She understood that the institution of the Blessed Sacrament cost her Son the greatest price. Her Jesus died in order to save us and remain with us in the Sacred Host. Thus, it breaks her maternal heart when she sees her Eucharistic Son treated poorly, mocked, blasphemed, received unworthily, or neglected in his tabernacles. As a mother, she longs to feed her children with the Bread that gives eternal life. She wants her children to be happy and blessed. She knows that this only happens through the Eucharistic Jesus.

> Immaculate Mother, who so carefully kept and ruminated in your heart what you heard and knew about your Jesus, multiply the souls that do not speak, nor act, nor feel, nor think more than ruminating on the good that your Jesus gives them in the tabernacle.[6]
>
> — St. Manuel González García

A mother can't give what a mother doesn't have. Mary has the Eucharist, and her greatest desire is that everyone know and love him. She made the Body and Blood of Jesus. She wants us to receive this gift, treasure this gift, and adore this gift. Mary's Eucharistic life is an inspiration to all of us to live a Eucharistic life as she did. Her example shows us that you don't have to be a priest or a deacon to do it. All

Christians are called to it: children, teens, boys, girls, men, women, widows, and everyone. God himself desires that all who place themselves under the headship of Jesus Christ acknowledge the Real Presence of Jesus in the Blessed Sacrament and live a Eucharistic life. This is the way to happiness on earth and joy in heaven!

> Undoubtedly, it was particularly for you, Mary, that Jesus instituted the Sacrament of Love. If he was not willing to leave us orphans when he ascended into heaven, how could he abandon you in exile without living at your side, without leaving you his body, his soul, his heart, and his divinity during the years of your solitude on earth? Obtain for us today, from Jesus, that he might pour out, over those of us who love him so much in the Eucharist, all the blessings that he sends to the world by means of the consecrated Host.[7]
>
> — Blessed Concepción Cabrera de Armida

Reflection Questions

1. How can you imitate Our Lady and live a more a Eucharistic life?
2. What are some practical ways you can make the Holy Eucharist your only possession, glory, and joy?
3. How can you make Jesus in the Blessed Sacrament more known to others?

Resolution

Today, ask Our Lady, Mother of the Eucharist, to intercede for you and make your life more Eucharistic. Ask her for the grace to make the Eucharist the center of your life.

Prayer

Dear Jesus, my Eucharistic Lord, enlighten my heart so that I can live a more Eucharistic life. Help me to be more like the Virgin Mary in my love for you. Give me courage and help me to never do anything that is against your will. Our Lady of the Most Blessed Sacrament, help me to live a life of hiddenness in God as you did. Keep me always fixed on our Eucharistic Lord. Saint Joseph, help me to be more like Mary in desiring the Blessed Sacrament to be more known and loved. Saint Peter Julian Eymard, Apostle of the Eucharist, fill me with your Eucharistic zeal so that I might love the Blessed Sacrament above all things.

Pray the Litany of the Most Precious Blood (page 166)

DAY 19
Mary's Interior Life

Retreat Master: St. Peter Julian Eymard

Faithful to her motherly mission, Mary will educate souls by showing them our Lord in the Eucharist, by sharing with them her own piety, her devotedness to worship, by forming in them the virtues necessary to the Eucharistic life. Things must be so, for it is evident to me that the only true devotion to the Eucharist will be found in souls formed by Mary.[1]

Let us study a few aspects of this life of our mother at the foot of the Blessed Sacrament. Mary adored the Eucharist with a most submissive faith. She adored her divine son hidden, veiled under a strange form.[2]

Mary's adoration was profound, interior, intimate. It was the gift of herself. She offered her whole self to the service of love of the Eucharistic God. For love lays down no conditions, makes no reservations; it thinks no longer of self, lives no longer for self; it is a stranger to itself and lives only for God which it loves. Everything in Mary was directed to the Blessed Sacrament as to its center and end.[3]

Eucharistic adorers share Mary's life and mission of prayer at the foot of the Most Blessed Sacrament. It is the most beautiful of all missions, and it holds no perils. It is the most holy, for in it all the virtues are practiced. It is, moreover, the most necessary to the Church, which has even more need of prayerful souls than of powerful preachers; of men of penance rather than of men of eloquence. Today more than ever have we need of men who by their self-immolation, disarm the anger of God inflamed by the ever-increasing crimes of nations. We must have souls who by their importunity re-open the treasures of grace which the indifference of the multitude has closed. We must have true adorers; that is to say, men of fervor and of sacrifice.[4]

Reflection

Mary will educate souls by showing them our Lord in the Eucharist.

She offered her whole self to the service of love of the Eucharistic God.

Eucharistic adorers share Mary's life and mission of prayer.

If you want to live a Eucharistic life, you must imitate the perfect adorer of the Holy Eucharist, the Immaculate Mother of God. Every saint knows that true devotion to Mary fosters adoration of Jesus in the Holy Eucharist. The Virgin Mary desires to feed all her spiritual children with the heavenly bread that was formed in her holy womb. As the New Eve and mother of all the living, she wants to prepare her spiritual children for worthy reception of Jesus Eucharistic. She also wants us to adore him and make reparation to him in the Blessed Sacrament.

After the Ascension of Jesus, Mary had to adjust to Jesus' new way of being present to her. He was now hidden from view under the veil of the Eucharist. This way of being with Jesus requires great faith, trust, love, and an intense interior life. Naturally, as his mother, Mary would have missed and longed for the physical, visible presence of her Jesus; his eyes, voice, smile, laughter, and facial features. Yet by faith she knew that her dearest Jesus was just as present to her in the Eucharist as he was in the cradle in Bethlehem and in their home in Nazareth. As Mother of the Church and spiritual mother to all the disciples of Jesus, Mary desires to teach all her spiritual children that they too can trust that Jesus is truly present in the Eucharist and put full confidence in knowing that he is with them in this hidden manner.

How greatly Mary desires to teach her spiritual children

about the necessity of living an interior Eucharistic life and being properly disposed to receive her Son in Holy Communion. It is no wonder that our Retreat Master stated that "the best preparation for Communion is the one that is made through Mary."[5] The Blessed Mother's entire life was a preparation for Holy Communion. It is by imitating her and seeking her assistance that we are able to receive her son as he desires to be received, with the utmost reverence, faith, humility, and love.

Our Lady teaches us that receiving Jesus in Holy Communion and being with him in adoration is the greatest of all gifts and the most necessary mission in the Church. At this critical time in the world and in the Church, when so few souls believe in the Real Presence, daily bombarded with distractions and diversions that take us away from the Eucharist, Our Lady teaches us about the importance of living an interior life. Without an interior life, we cannot lead Eucharistic lives. Without an interior life, we run the risk of becoming busybodies, too preoccupied with action, too involved in the things of the world to prepare for Holy Mass, and too consumed with tasks to spend time in adoration before the Blessed Sacrament.

Our Lady helped transformed the world through her prayers, penances, and love for Jesus in the Eucharist. We must follow her selfless example and set the world aflame with love for Jesus Eucharistic.

> May the kingdom of your Eucharistic Heart come
> to us through your Immaculate Mother![6]
> —St. Manuel González García

Reflection Questions

1. How is Mary, your spiritual mother, a model for Eucharistic adoration?
2. In what areas of your Eucharistic devotion can you strive to be more like Our Lady?
3. How can Mary's selfless interior life help you in your preparation and reception of Holy Communion?

Resolution

Today, ask Our Lady to give you a share in the spiritual intimacy that she shares with Jesus in the Blessed Sacrament. Ask her for the grace to imitate her, live an interior life, and help you become an adorer of the Holy Eucharist.

Prayer

Dear Jesus, my Eucharistic Lord, teach me to be more like Mary. I pray for the grace of an interior Eucharistic life. Like Mary, I want to live for you alone and never be far from you. Our Lady of the Most Blessed Sacrament, help me to always receive our Lord with devotion, piety, and faith. Saint Joseph, instruct me in the ways of prayer, adoration, and the interior life. Saint Peter Julian Eymard, Apostle of the Eucharist, fill me with your Eucharistic zeal so that I might love the Blessed Sacrament above all things.

Pray the Litany of the Holy Eucharist (page 163)

DAY 20
Mary's Sacrificial Life

Retreat Master: St. Peter Julian Eymard

It was in sharing the immolation of Jesus in the Most Blessed Sacrament that the strength of Mary's soul and the perfection of her conforming with Jesus were greatest.[1]

In order to appreciate the gift of the Eucharist, the adorer ought to go as Mary did, and with her, to its sources, to the sacrifices it demanded of our Lord's love. If that love is beautiful on Calvary, it is even more beautiful on the Altar, for there it is love forever immolated. The contemplation of those sufferings and of that victory will suggest to the adorer what he owes in return to a God so good. Then, with Mary, the adorer will offer himself to Jesus Eucharistic with his whole heart, to bless him, to thank him for so much love. He will devote himself to honoring the various states of our Sacramental Jesus, practicing in his life those virtues that the Savior continues and glorifies so admirably therein. He will honor the profound humility of the Savior which goes so far as to annihilate himself entirely under the Sacred Species. He will honor the abnegation of his power and glory which makes him the prisoner of men. He will honor his obedience, which makes him the servant of all. He will take Mary as the pattern of his Eucharistic life in order to aid him in his practical study. He will love her and confide himself to her as to the Mother of adorers.[2]

Reflection

With Mary, the adorer will offer himself to Jesus Eucharistic. He will take Mary as the pattern of his Eucharistic life. He will love her and confide himself to her.

Our Retreat Master wants you to adore the Eucharist. As the "Apostle of the Eucharist," he wants to teach you how to model your life of adoration after that of Our Lady. To do this, sacrificial love is required. Adoring Jesus in the manger of Bethlehem is easy. Even nominal Christians adore Jesus in this fashion once a year. What requires great love and sacrifice is adoring and imitating the self-emptying love at Calvary and in the Holy Eucharist.

Mary will teach you how to do it. She will teach you that adoring and imitating Jesus in the Eucharist, lacking any tangible awareness of his presence, helps you become virtuous and holy because the Eucharist is a school of trust. If you lack trust in Jesus, God himself can do very little for you. Did Jesus not tell St. Faustina Kowalska that the one vessel that opens the floodgates of heavenly graces is trust? Trust, and the willingness to suffer for love, is what unlocks the power to conquer all things. There is no greater lesson of how to live sacrificial, self-emptying love than in the Blessed Sacrament.

In recent times, many Catholics have fallen into the snares of the prosperity-type Gospel. A Gospel promising earthly wealth and pleasures, devoid of the Cross, suffering, and sacrificial love. In such a Gospel, faith is magical and whimsical, suffering and sacrifice are to be avoided and shunned at every opportunity. Yet this is a false Gospel and something completely foreign to the Virgin Mary and a true follower of Jesus. A faithful disciple of Jesus desires to love, adore, and imitate Jesus in all his virtues as witnessed in Bethlehem, Egypt, Nazareth, Jerusalem, the Upper Room, Gethsemane, Calvary, the Mass, and in the tabernacle. This is what Mary did. It is what we are called to do because it brings about tremendous fruit for ourselves and for the world.

Each time that Mary, my most Holy Mother, felt the pain of my absence in whatever form, she immediately offered it to the Father for the salvation of the world and of the newborn Church. This

apostolate of suffering in Mary, during this period
of solitude, was the most fertile and caused heaven
to pour itself out in graces.[3]

— Jesus to Blessed Concepción Cabrera de Armida

Self-denial and sacrifice are part and parcel of the Christian life. Whether adoring Jesus at Mass or in the tabernacle, adorers of Jesus are called to be co-redeemers with Christ as Mary is Co-Redemptrix with Christ. We are called to suffer for, and in union with, Jesus. Our Lady's suffering did not end after Jesus rose from the dead and ascended to his Father. On the contrary, her suffering continued because her love for God and mankind continued. She desired the glory of God and the salvation of souls. All her prayer, mortification, and penances were done for mankind out of love. She brought all her sufferings and intentions to each Communion she received. All her sufferings were united to her Eucharistic Lord.

The same should be the case with you. You should desire to be always united to Christ in the Eucharist and offer up all your suffering, penances, and mortifications to our Eucharistic Lord out of love for God and the salvation of souls. If you love much, and are willing to suffer, you will be blessed. Those who are willing to love very little are willing to suffer very little too.

Are you willing to offer all your suffering out of love for Jesus and souls? You have a model and a mother in Our Lady. Jesus wants you to participate in his redemptive work and be so united with his Eucharistic love that you become another Mary, an *altera Maria*, for him and for others. Don't be afraid of love. Don't be afraid of suffering. Look to Our Lady and imitate her fervor for the Eucharist. She will give you the strength and zeal to make great sacrifices for God and for souls.

Reflection Questions

1. How can you imitate Mary in living a more sacrificial life in union with the Holy Eucharist?
2. Is there something you can offer to Jesus in the Blessed Sacrament for his glory and the good of souls?
3. Who are some saints who lived sacrificial Eucharistic lives?

Resolution

Today, join your prayers to those of Mary. Ask God to make you more sacrificial so that he may be glorified and souls may be saved. Implore the Blessed Mother to bring back many sinners to Jesus, especially those who have turned away from belief in his Real Presence.

Prayer

Dear Jesus, my Eucharistic Lord, I love you and want to make greater sacrifices for you. Like Mary, I want my heart to be aflame with love for your glory and the salvation of souls. Our Lady of the Most Blessed Sacrament, help me to sacrifice myself and offer all my sufferings to Jesus in the Eucharist for the salvation of souls. Saint Joseph, give me a share of the love of your Most Chaste Heart for Jesus. Saint Peter Julian Eymard, Apostle of the Eucharist, fill me with your Eucharistic zeal so that I might love the Blessed Sacrament above all things.

Pray the Litany of the Most Precious Blood (page 166)

DAY 21
St. Joseph, the Humble Adorer

Retreat Master: St. Peter Julian Eymard

Saint Joseph was the first adorer, the first religious. Although he never adored our Lord under the Eucharistic species and never had the happiness of communicating [receiving Holy Communion], he did possess and adore Jesus in human form.

Saint Joseph knew our Lord more thoroughly than did all the saints together; he lived for him alone. In that lies his special glory, the keynote of his sanctity. In that, above all, he is our model, and in that too does his incomparable greatness consist.[1]

We can hardly imagine his feelings of humility in seeing the Incarnate Word reduced almost to the state of a slave, and in hearing Mary call herself his humble servant.

Humility must be the dominant virtue of an adorer. Like St. Joseph, the adorer must consider himself unworthy of serving Jesus. He must honor Christ's Eucharistic abasements by giving up all self-glory, all self-esteem, everything that might draw admiration upon himself.

The great rule must be that of St. Joseph who never appears when there is a question of glory in the service of Jesus, and that of St. John the Baptist who, in answer to praise, cried out: "He must increase, I must decrease" (Jn 3:30).[2]

Reflection

Saint Joseph was the first adorer.

He is our model.

Humility must be the dominant virtue of an adorer.

Our Retreat Master states that St. Joseph was the first

adorer of Jesus. Wouldn't the first adorer of Jesus be Mary? There's an easy answer to this question. In Catholicism, Mary is understood to be so great in dignity that we only refer to her as a saint when we are describing a building or an institution named after her. For example, "St. Mary's Hospital" or "St. Mary's Parochial School." Catholics rarely address Our Lady as "St. Mary." She is the Mother of God and in a category of holiness all her own. What our Retreat Master means, therefore, is that St. Joseph is the first *saint* to adore Jesus.

During his earthly life, St. Joseph never had the privilege of adoring Jesus in Eucharistic form or receiving our Lord in Holy Communion, but he adored the Body, Blood, Soul, and Divinity of Christ on a daily basis. After Mary, St. Joseph offers us the greatest example of adoring Jesus. In a certain sense, St. Joseph was the forerunner of Eucharistic adoration. This humble saint preferred a life of adoration and obscurity, a life of intimacy with Jesus and Mary, rather than a life of recognition and notoriety. He is, after Christ, the humblest of all men. He did everything for God's greater glory and shunned the praises of men. He desired to do the will of the Heavenly Father and imitate the hiddenness of God's Divine Paternity. His humble dwellings in Egypt and Nazareth were akin to adoration chapels. He lived for Jesus and Mary and was the man closest to the Real Presence. He is the greatest of all the saints and shared daily life in the presence of the Body, Blood, Soul, and Divinity of Jesus Christ.

In order to grow in humility, we need to imitate St. Joseph's hidden life, as well as his desire to live for Jesus and adore Jesus. In modern times, is God not revealing the greatness of St. Joseph in extraordinary ways? From December 8, 2020, to December 8, 2021, the Catholic Church celebrated a Year of St. Joseph, the only year dedicated to St. Joseph in the history of the Church! New books, statues, paintings, pilgrimages, shrines, and organizations have come into existence, emphasizing the humility, love, dignity, and intercessory power of St. Joseph. The best thing we can do to honor St. Joseph is imitate him, especially his adoration of Jesus.

As our spiritual father, St. Joseph is worthy of imitation. We should strive to acquire his virtues and his adoration of the Body, Blood, Soul, and Divinity of Jesus. His fatherly example teaches us to be silent, humble, loving, sacrificial, and centered on the Real Presence.

With his immaculate bride, St. Joseph desires nothing more than to lead all souls to Jesus, especially the mystery of the Holy Eucharist. If you think about it, we would not have the Eucharist without St. Joseph. Our Lady cooperated with God materially to bring about the Incarnation by her *Fiat*. The Second Person of the Blessed Trinity took on flesh and assumed human nature in her womb. Saint Joseph, on the other hand, cooperated in the Incarnation in his role as husband of Mary and protector of the Heavenly Bread (Jesus). He especially did this when the life of Jesus was threatened by Herod. The Virgin Mary made the Heavenly Bread in her womb, but St. Joseph guarded and preserved the Heavenly Bread for all future generations.

Do you remember the story of the Patriarch Joseph from the Old Testament, the one sold into slavery by his brothers and taken to Egypt to be of service to Pharaoh? The Patriarch Joseph interpreted Pharaoh's dreams and was so favored that Pharaoh put him in charge of all the granaries (storehouses of bread) in Egypt. Then, when a famine struck the known world, everyone went to Joseph for bread. Pharaoh himself told those in search of food, "Go to Joseph" (Genesis 41:55). Well, that was all a preparation, a prototype, for a much greater Joseph with a much greater Bread!

Saint Joseph, the humble adorer, has been put in charge of guarding and protecting the Heavenly Manna so that you can have eternal life by receiving it. This is what a good father does for his children. Saint Joseph never received the Heavenly Manna in Eucharistic form himself, but as a good and humble father, he protected and preserved the Heavenly Bread for you!

> Let us go to the new Joseph. Let us give him the homage of a sincere devotion. Let us cast ourselves into his arms, then, as in olden times the children of Jacob cast themselves into the arms of their brother. Just as the older Joseph comforted them in their needs and loaded them with gifts, the new Joseph will care for us. "Go to Joseph, and do all that he shall say to you" (Gen 41:55). Let us cry for mercy to St. Joseph, and he will open the granaries of grace to enrich us.[3]
>
> — Blessed Basil Moreau

> Pharaoh, the mighty king of Egypt, exalted Joseph and made him the highest prince in his kingdom, because he stored up the grain and bread and saved the people of his entire kingdom. So Joseph saved and protected Christ, who is the living bread and gives eternal life to the world.[4]
>
> — St. Lawrence of Brindisi

> Saint Joseph most diligently reared him whom the faithful were to receive as the bread that came down from heaven whereby they might obtain eternal life.[5]
>
> — Blessed Pope Pius IX

> Keeping in mind the great patriarch Joseph, sold by his brothers in Egypt, understand that our saint has inherited not only his name, but even more, his power, his innocence, and his sanctity. As the patriarch Joseph stored the wheat not for himself, but for the people in their time of need, so Joseph has received a heavenly commission to watch over

the living Bread not for himself alone, but for the entire world.[6]

— St. Bernard of Clairvaux

Saint Joseph is still charged with guarding the Living Bread![7]

— Venerable Fulton J. Sheen

Reflection Questions

1. How can St. Joseph's humility help you grow in humility?
2. In what ways did St. Joseph adore Jesus?
3. How can you live a saintly life without seeking the praise of others?

Resolution

Today, ask St. Joseph to help you grow in humility. Implore the Most Chaste Heart of St. Joseph for the gift of being an adorer of Christ and a servant of Mary Immaculate.

Prayer

Dear Jesus, my Eucharistic Lord, thank you for the good spiritual father you have given me in St. Joseph. He raised you and saved you from Herod so that we could receive you as the Heavenly Manna that gives us eternal life. Please make my heart as humble and self-sacrificing as the Most Chaste Heart of St. Joseph. Our Lady of the Most Blessed Sacrament, intercede that I might be hidden and humble like you. Saint Joseph, humble adorer of Christ, I want to imitate and be like you. I love you, St. Joseph. Saint Peter Julian Eymard, Apostle of the Eucharist, fill me with your Eucharistic zeal so that I might love the Blessed Sacrament above all things.

Pray the Litany of the Holy Eucharist (page 163)

DAY 22
St. Joseph, the Perpetual Adorer

Retreat Master: St. Peter Julian Eymard

As foster-father of Jesus and husband of Mary, Joseph ranks among the elite of heaven. On earth he deserves the same recognition, for his mission, which will last as long as the Church itself, draws everyone within its scope. As adorers we have a right to a large share of his graces and protection, and careful study will show that all his special gifts and graces aimed at making him a good adorer.

From his entry into the world, even while still enclosed in Mary's womb as in a living ciborium, Jesus singled out Mary and Joseph to be his adorers. Joseph responded royally; he never ceased adoring Jesus in her womb. And after the Child's birth at Bethlehem, Joseph and Mary adored him uninterruptedly as he lay before their eyes. They represented all mankind at the feet of Christ. Certainly Adam and Eve were well replaced!

At Nazareth, Joseph's days were filled with work which necessarily took him away at times from his Infant God. During these hours Mary replaced him, but when evening brought him home again, he would pass the entire night in adoration, never tiring, only too happy for the chance to contemplate the hidden riches of Jesus' divinity. For he pierced the rough garments the child wore, until his faith touched the Sacred Heart. In profound adoration he united himself to the special grace of each one of the events in the life of Jesus. He adored our Lord in his hidden life and in his Passion and death; he adored in advance the Eucharistic Christ in his tabernacles. There was nothing that our Lord could hide from St. Joseph.

Among the graces which Jesus gave to his foster-father — and he flooded him with the graces attached to every one of his mysteries — is that special grace given to an adorer of the Blessed Sacrament. That is the one we must ask of St. Joseph. Have confidence, strong confidence in him. Take him as the patron and the model of your life of adoration.[1]

Reflection

Jesus singled out Mary and Joseph to be his adorers.

They represented all of mankind at the feet of Christ.

Saint Joseph is the patron and the model of your life of adoration.

Saint Joseph was a perpetual adorer of Jesus. He first adored him hidden behind the immaculate veil of Mary's holy womb. Next, he adored Jesus in the cave of Bethlehem, the world's first public adoration chapel. When St. Joseph was commanded by the angel to flee from Herod and take his wife and son to Egypt, he adored Jesus in pagan territory. When the Holy Family returned to Nazareth after being in Egypt for many years, St. Joseph daily adored Jesus for decades. Whether on family outings to Jerusalem, visitations to relatives, or walking about in the countryside, St. Joseph never ceased adoring Jesus. He is the perpetual and model adorer.

In a certain sense, St. Joseph is the founder of adoration chapels. Wherever he traveled with his wife and son, his paternal leadership transformed the home into an adoration chapel. He is the first to conduct a procession with the Body and Blood of Christ when he fled to Egypt with his infant Son. He is also the model for nocturnal adorers, that is, those who adore our Lord during the night. In all these things, St. Joseph offers us a superb model of how to adore Jesus.

What makes St. Joseph our model of adoration is his great faith. His faith pierced the veil of heaven and beheld mysteries beyond human comprehension on a daily basis. What mysteries must have been revealed to him as he adored Jesus asleep at his feet, at the family table, and as Jesus received a thousand kisses from his immaculate mother. Saint Joseph's adoration of Jesus must have born tremendous fruit and flooded his chaste heart with indescribable graces. These graces were not for him alone, but for all his spiritual children because St. Joseph is our spiritual father. Is he not worthy of our imitation? Saint Joseph provides for us a most worthy model of how to live in perpetual adoration of Jesus.

Undoubtedly, St. Joseph reached the heights of union with God because of his adoration of Jesus. This mystical union with God is not reserved for Mary, St. Joseph, monks, and nuns, but for all people who cooperate with grace. Imitate St. Joseph and be his faithful spiritual child and you, too, will be capable of intimate union with God. Place yourself daily at the feet of Jesus and adore him.

Before the sun, we become tan, but before the Eucharistic Jesus, we become holy.[2]

— Blessed Carlo Acutis

Reflection Questions

1. When was the last time you invoked St. Joseph to help you increase your love for the Eucharist?
2. How can St. Joseph teach you to become a better adorer of Christ?
3. What graces can you ask St. Joseph to give you that will help you be more like him?

Resolution

Today, pray to St. Joseph and ask him to give you the grace to live a life of perpetual adoration of our Lord. Request that your heart become more like his Most Chaste Heart, especially his love for the hidden Jesus.

Prayer

Dear Jesus, my Eucharistic Lord, I thank you for all the graces you have poured out in the Holy Eucharist. Thank you for your virginal father, St. Joseph, who, after Mary, loved you more than anyone on earth. Our Lady of the Most Blessed Sacrament, help me to be more like St. Joseph and adore Jesus at all times. Saint Joseph, draw me closer to the Blessed Sacrament, instruct me in the mysteries of Christ, and help me to be, like you, a perpetual adorer of Jesus. Saint Peter Julian Eymard, Apostle of the Eucharist, fill me with your Eucharistic zeal so that I might love the Blessed Sacrament above all things.

Pray the Litany of the Most Precious Blood (page 166)

DAY 23
St. Joseph, the Poor Adorer

Retreat Master: St. Peter Julian Eymard

The Word of God, desiring to espouse our poor humanity, became poor for love of us.

Saint Joseph, therefore, who was to have the glorious title and power of foster-father of Jesus, had then to add evangelical poverty to all his qualities and royal glory. The religious vows have come down to us from Nazareth, the original monastery, where poverty, chastity, and obedience were first practiced. There St. Joseph practiced all the counsels; and, though foster-father of Jesus, he was his most humble disciple.

Saint Joseph was poor in the goods of this world. He possessed nothing in Bethlehem, the country where his ancestors had been kings. He lived in Nazareth, the poorest and most despised of cities. And the house where the Incarnate Word was conceived, to whom did that belong? We do not know. But judging from what we see at Loreto, how poor and cramped it was!

Saint Joseph had no personal resources, but was obliged to live by his trade, a lowly trade, that of a carpenter. His clothes (as is provided by his mantle, which is still preserved as a sacred relic) were poor and plain like those worn by other men of his rank. His food was that of the poor: his daily bread was barley bread.

Really it is almost shocking to see the Eternal Father send his son into the midst of such great poverty. He knew that: yet he willed it, and it was he himself who had reduced St. Joseph to such dire straits. He willed that from the first moment his son should repair our attachment to material goods and our abuse of riches. So there was St. Joseph, who by right of birth might have been a king — there he was, an ordinary carpenter, looking so insignificant that all of Bethlehem rejected him and relegated him to the meanest of shelters, a stable.

But St. Joseph had the spirit and the grace of Jesus Christ's poverty. He was happy to share it; he preferred it to all the wealth and glory of this world.

Like St. Joseph, Eucharistic souls should esteem, cherish, and practice holy poverty, be content with the necessities of life, and find in poverty the means of offering a sacrifice to the royal poverty of the Eucharistic God.[1]

Reflection

Saint Joseph had the spirit and the grace of Jesus Christ's poverty.

By right of birth, St. Joseph might have been a king.

Like St. Joseph, be content with the necessities of life.

Are you shocked that our Retreat Master states that you must be poor? Is he saying that you have to give away all your possessions? No, that is not what he is saying. Our Retreat Master is reminding us of an essential aspect of living an authentic Christian life, namely, we must be detached from all material things. Jesus is our treasure. This is the heart, the essence, of what it means to live the virtue of poverty. God has given us the greatest example of living holy poverty in the Blessed Sacrament.

God's self-emptying love is perfectly expressed in the poverty of the Eucharist. He has emptied himself of everything, hidden under the veil of a piece of bread, so that you can become spiritually rich. When you gaze upon the Sacred Host, Jesus reminds you that he is your daily bread and your all. Come what may, the poverty of Eucharistic Love teaches you to be content with the necessities of life. Jesus is enough for you. Saint Joseph teaches us that Jesus is our supreme treasure. Material things come and go, but God never changes.

In St. Joseph, we find an example of what can be called "Eucharistic poverty," that is, living only for the Real Presence of Jesus and leaving everything else to divine providence. Let's unpack what "Eucharistic poverty" looked like for St. Joseph.

Saint Joseph was unpretentious in the eyes of the world. He had no worldly ambition or desire for recognition. He was happy with his daily bread, that is, Jesus. People have often wondered what the financial status of the Holy Family was, or what their living conditions were. We need only look in the New Testament to find out. The Holy Family was poor. Very poor. Saint Joseph was so poor that his wife had to give birth in a place reserved for animals. Then, when the Holy Family journeyed to the Temple in Jerusalem to participate in the Jewish ritual of purification for a new mother, St. Joseph couldn't even afford to purchase a lamb for a burnt offering (see Leviticus 12:6–7). Lambs were expensive. He could only afford a poor man's gift, that is, two turtledoves or two young pigeons (see Leviticus 12:8).

Saint Joseph lived on Divine Providence. Had Baby Jesus not been given gold, frankincense, and myrrh by the Wise Men in Bethlehem, it is likely that the Head of the Holy Family would not have had money to purchase food and other necessities for his family when they fled to Egypt. After all, when they journeyed from Nazareth to Bethlehem to fulfill the census, they did not bring many things with them because they expected to return to Nazareth immediately. The gifts of the Wise Men were God's providential way of taking care of the Holy Family during their initial sojourn in Egypt. Years later, after returning to Nazareth from Egypt, the Holy Family lived for almost 30 years in a house in Nazareth that was simple and small.

"Blessed are the poor in spirit, for theirs is the kingdom of heaven" (Matthew 5:3). Have you ever wondered what Jesus meant by that statement? Is Jesus saying that poverty is wonderful and everyone should give away everything they have and live in a tent? No, that's not what our Lord is saying. What he is saying is that those who are detached from the things of this world are not far from the Kingdom of Heaven because they rely on Divine Providence. When a person is detached from the things of this world, poverty is understood to be a virtue. The person who is detached from material things is truly blessed in spirit and rich in the sight of God. This explains why St. Joseph is called "Lover of Poverty." He relied on Divine Providence for all his needs. He lived, worked, and died for Jesus.

Saint Joseph will teach you how to be detached from material things and abandoned to Divine Providence. You will never find true happiness in material goods. When you allow your relationship with God to be dependent upon whether you have material things, you are headed for unhappiness. The person who is poor in spirit, on the other hand, is able to proclaim, "The Lord gave and the Lord has taken away; blessed be the name of the Lord" (Job 1:21).

Live for the Eucharist!

Reflection Questions

1. What is your attitude toward holy poverty? Do you understand it correctly?
2. How can you imitate St. Joseph's poverty?
3. How can you imitate St. Joseph's trust in Divine Providence and living for Jesus?

Resolution

Today, speak to the Lord from the poverty of your heart and ask him to give you a spirit of detachment from the things of this world. Make an act of trust in Divine Providence and desire to imitate St. Joseph and his boundless trust in God.

Prayer

Dear Jesus, my Eucharistic Lord, I thank you for becoming poor, so that I might learn poverty of spirit. Thank you for your virginal father, St. Joseph, who taught you the importance of relying on Divine Providence. Our Lady of the Most Blessed Sacrament, help me to be content with whatever God gives me. Saint Joseph, poor adorer of Jesus, you lived for Jesus, help me to prefer the Eucharist to all the passing things of this world. Saint Peter Julian Eymard, Apostle of the Eucharist, fill me with your Eucharistic zeal so that I might love the Blessed Sacrament above all things.

Pray the Litany of the Holy Eucharist (page 163)

DAY 24
The Holy Angels

Retreat Master: St. Peter Julian Eymard

At every instant, millions of angels go forth and return to the tabernacle after having accomplished his orders. The tabernacle is their center, their head-quarters, for there they find the Commander-in-Chief of the celestial army. Do you see? Do you understand? All creatures obey him, and we know nothing of it. See how he knows to conceal his action! See how he knows to command in annihilation![1]

We must grow nearer to the divine tabernacle and live there unnoticed like the angels do.[2]

Continue to serve our Lord in the holy and adorable Eucharist, like the angels serve him in heaven and on earth.[3]

Live by the divine Eucharist and for the divine Eucharist, like the angels who live only for God in heaven.[4]

What do the angels and saints need to make them happy? God, Jesus Christ. Well! We have him, we are with him, we are at his gracious service![5]

It is proper that adorers who fulfill the same ministry as the angels near their heavenly King should shine with outstanding purity.[6]

Stay at the feet of the Blessed Sacrament like the angels, and let the world be agitated like straw in a whirlwind.[7]

Reflection

Millions of angels go forth and return to the tabernacle.

The tabernacle is their center.

Live for the divine Eucharist like the angels.

Daily, millions of angels carry out our Lord's orders

from his throne in heaven and from his Real Presence in the tabernacle. As our Retreat Master states, Jesus is Commander-in-Chief of the celestial armies. All the holy angels serve him, praise him, adore him, and fight for him. The tabernacle is the holy angels' headquarters.

Is the tabernacle your headquarters?

> It is in our churches, in this tabernacle, that the living Body of the Savior rests. He was but nine months in the womb of Mary, three hours on the cross, three days in the tomb. Yet he is always in our churches. This is why they do not empty of angels, archangels, and seraphim unceasingly adoring him.[8]
>
> — St. Claude de la Colombière

Many saints have claimed to see angels during the Holy Sacrifice of the Mass and during Eucharistic adoration. The angels are God's servants and do his holy will. They pass unnoticed before our eyes, yet, when we attend Holy Mass or Eucharistic adoration, we are surrounded by armies of holy angels. They have no self-interest; their one desire is to serve and worship God. Like soldiers on a battlefield, they fight for God and constantly await their marching orders. It should be the same for you.

Our Retreat Master had a great love for the angels and prayed to them frequently, asking for their protection and powerful intercession. He was particularly devoted to St. Michael the Archangel. This great angel is a dragon slayer. His name in Hebrew means "Who is like God." Our Retreat Master once said the following about St. Michael the Archangel: "Let us honor him well. He is the soldier of God's glory."[9] If you do not know the Prayer to St. Michael the Archangel, you should learn it and pray it frequently.

> Saint Michael the Archangel, defend us in battle. Be our protection against the wickedness and snares of

the devil; May God rebuke him, we humbly pray; And do thou, O Prince of the Heavenly Host, by the power of God, cast into hell Satan and all the evil spirits who prowl about the world seeking the ruin of souls. Amen.

Many people recite the Prayer to St. Michael after Holy Mass. It is a wonderful and praiseworthy practice. When you say this prayer, you invoke an extremely powerful archangel who stands watch before God and is always ready to defend you against the wickedness and snares of the devil.

All the holy angels are filled with awe before the Blessed Sacrament because God conceals himself in such a humble manner. Yet, as great as the angels are, they are not able to receive Holy Communion. They do not have bodies. They can only receive Jesus spiritually. What amazement the holy angels must have as they witness human creatures receive our Lord in Holy Communion. Yet what horror must fill their being as they witness men and women receiving Holy Communion unworthily, as well as when the Holy Eucharist is mocked, ridiculed, desecrated, and profaned.

Where would a holy angel want the tabernacle to be located in a Catholic church? Would a holy angel want it in a room distant from the sanctuary, out of sight of the people in the pews? What about behind a wall where no one can see it? No, only fallen angels would desire the tabernacle to be located in such places. Holy angels desire the tabernacle in every parish be in the sanctuary. They know well that the first tabernacle of the Real Presence was the holy womb of the Virgin Mary. Her body serves as the template for tabernacle placement in all Catholic churches. In the sanctuary.

If you are a bishop or a priest, you can do something great for God and his people. You can establish a never-ending Eucharistic revival in your diocese and parish, making an everlasting impact in the hearts of the faithful, by placing the tabernacle back in the sanctuary.

Reflection Questions

1. How can you cultivate a better awareness of the angels' presence at Holy Mass and Eucharistic Adoration?
2. What lessons can the angels teach you about worshiping and serving our Lord?
3. What are the means you are taking to become a Eucharistic adorer like the angels?

Resolution

Today, ask your Guardian Angel to intercede for you before the Blessed Sacrament. Pray the Prayer to St. Michael the Archangel several times throughout the day and, over the next several weeks, try to memorize it.

Prayer

Dear Jesus, my Eucharistic Lord, I thank you for the gift of your holy angels. They adore you unceasingly and protect me from so many dangers. Help me to be more like them in adoring you. Our Lady of the Most Blessed Sacrament, Queen of Angels, help me to serve Jesus with greater zeal like the holy angels. Saint Joseph, help me to be pure like the holy angels and fully devoted to the Eucharist. Saint Peter Julian Eymard, Apostle of the Eucharist, fill me with your Eucharistic zeal so that I might love the Blessed Sacrament above all things.

Pray the Litany of the Most Precious Blood (page 166)

DAY 25
The Cross

Retreat Master: St. Peter Julian Eymard

The Cross comes from God.

The good Master visits us now and then with the grace of Calvary, but also with the strength of his love. It is a comfort to see this love of God sweetening the Cross. It is necessary for the Cross, this good daughter of heaven, to come to us; otherwise we should always remain on Mount Tabor. But nothing lasts very long; and the sun is more beautiful after the storm or after emerging from the clouds which veil it.

Be convinced of this: the state of suffering always comes from God. It is the state he chooses for our greater good and for the sake of granting us some very special grace. And so if you have suffered for some time, do not give way to discouragement but lift up your morale by trusting in God. Esteem yourself fortunate to suffer what this good Master sends you in his love for you. Praise God since in his goodness he gives you the most precious and loving thing he has, the proof of his love.[1]

Do not count the thorns. Do not let yourself be depressed or even worried by all these trials you are undergoing; they are only graces and helps to an even greater union with the Sovereign Good.

Fortify yourself well in the love of Jesus Christ and in what are the real tests of love for him, that is, the Cross, detachment from creatures, immolation of self to his greater glory, and you will feel as it were a new life in you, an ocean of peace, a need to suffer by way of requiting divine love and adding fuel to its fire. You will accomplish nothing lasting if you pay too much attention to the bad weather or cloudy skies. Rise above them to the sun which does not change place and dispenses light and heat to everything that revolves around it. Accept your crosses as so many changes in the weather and remain in peace with the grace of God.[2]

Reflection

It is necessary for the Cross to come to us.

Do not let yourself be depressed.

Fortify yourself well in the love of Jesus Christ.

The Cross, in a certain sense, can be considered as the spiritual wedding ring that Christ wears and gives to his bride, the Church. It is one of the best gifts that Jesus can give you because it is the sign of his committed and sacrificial love for you. By wearing this spiritual wedding band — the Cross — on your soul, the loving union between you and Christ is manifested to the world. As Jesus cannot be separated from his Cross because he is forever faithful, never taking off the spiritual wedding ring of the Cross, it should be the same with every Christian, that is, never abandoning, or taking off, the sign of his love. The Cross is the pledge of your commitment to Christ. If you take off the wedding ring of the Cross, there will be problems and most likely spiritual adultery and a chasing after false gods. If you do not embrace the Cross (wear the ring), you do not belong to Christ.

What spouse doesn't want to wear a wedding ring? What bride doesn't want a huge rock on her finger? The Cross is the ultimate "bling" in the spiritual life. It shows the world that you are loved and someone special to God. Jesus, the divine bridegroom and lover of our souls, invites you to wear the wedding ring of the Cross and follow him faithfully on the *Via Crucis* (the Way of the Cross): "If any man would come after me, let him deny himself and take up his cross daily and follow me" (Luke 9:23). If you truly love Christ you will want to wear the ring every day. Wearing it is not easy, but it is worth it. Suffering for love of Jesus is always worth it.

The Eucharist gives you the strength to carry the Cross and suffer with Christ. This is yet another reason why Satan hates the Eucharist and wants to take souls away from it. He knows that the Eucharist gives souls supernatural power to carry the cross, be faithful to Jesus, and willingly embrace suffering out of love for God and others. The Eucharist fortifies fidelity and makes you a saint.

Christianity without the Cross is not Christianity, and a person without a cross is not a Christian. To separate Christ from his Cross is to take Jesus' wedding ring away from him. He will never allow such action. Peter tried to do it, and Jesus had to rebuke him and call him Satan (see Matthew 16:23). As Christ was crucified out of love for you, you must also be willing to undergo crucifixion with him. It may not be a physical crucifixion, but it will most certainly be a spiritual and mystical crucifixion. How odd, then, that many Catholics today want nothing to do with the Cross. It is no wonder that belief in the Eucharist among Catholics is at an all-time low. When so few believe in his Real Presence in the Eucharist, it naturally follows that most no longer want to be committed to him and wear the spiritual wedding ring of the Cross. They have gone after false gods.

All Catholic prayers and devotions begin with the sign of the commitment, the Sign of the Cross. The Holy Mass begins this way and so do all truly Catholic prayers and devotions. In the Eucharist we find the strength to carry the Cross — wear the spiritual wedding ring — faithfully to the end "In the name of the Father, and of the Son, and of the Holy Spirit."

Wear the wedding ring of the Cross and never take it off.

The school of the saints is to be found in the Cross and in the Eucharist. This is where the soul is taught, where it learns, where it suffers, where it loves. This is where the soul retreats from the earth, where it draws near to heaven.[3]

— Jesus to Blessed Concepción Cabrera de Armida

Reflection Questions

1. How do you view suffering?
2. What are the greatest sufferings and crosses in your life?
3. How can your devotion to the Eucharist give you the strength to carry your cross and be faithful to Jesus Christ?

Resolution

Today, praise God for the gift of the Cross. Praise him for the gift of the spiritual wedding ring. Promise to love him in good times and in bad, in health and in sickness, in riches and in poverty, in life and in death.

Prayer

Dear Jesus, my Eucharistic Lord, I love you and thank you for the Cross. From this day forward, I want to wear it faithfully and never turn away from you. Help me to find strength to be faithful to you by being devoted to the Blessed Sacrament. Our Lady of the Most Blessed Sacrament, you stood firmly at the foot of the Cross and now stand before the tabernacle, grant me the grace to suffer with love, courage, and serenity. Saint Joseph, intercede for me that I truly understand the wisdom of the Cross and embrace it. Saint Peter Julian Eymard, Apostle of the Eucharist, fill me with your Eucharistic zeal so that I might love the Blessed Sacrament above all things.

Pray the Litany of the Holy Eucharist (page 163)

DAY 26
God's Goodness

Retreat Master: St. Peter Julian Eymard

What shall we say of the goodness of the God of the Eucharist! Ah! Lord! Yes, we must speak of the scandal of thy goodness! Jesus surrounds himself with weakness in the Blessed Sacrament. He allows himself to be insulted, disgraced, despised, profaned under his very eyes, in his very presence, at the very foot of his altar! And no angel is there to strike these Judases. None.

And the Heavenly Father allows his well-beloved Son to be insulted! This is worse than on Calvary. There at least the sun veiled itself for horror, and the universe mourned its Creator; but here, nothing! This Calvary of the Eucharist is set up everywhere. It started from the Cenacle and now covers the earth, and it will last to the last minute of the world's existence. O God! Why this excess?

This is the conflict of goodness with ingratitude. It is Jesus who wants to overcome man's hate with love, to love man in spite of himself, and to do him good. He will submit to anything rather than take revenge. He wants to wear out man's resistance with his goodness.[1]

Reflection

We must speak of the scandal of God's goodness.

Jesus surrounds himself with weakness in the Blessed Sacrament.

Jesus wants to overcome man's hate with love.

Our Retreat Master provides extraordinary insights into God's goodness and love. The goodness of God is so great that he is willing to be insulted and ignored in order to conquer us with his love. Think about it: World leaders and presidents of countries are surrounded by armies of guards to keep them safe and protect them from injury. Were a person to attack, insult, or mock them, they would be escorted away quickly and prosecuted. In the Holy Eucharist, however, the King of Kings and Lord of Lords allows himself to be insulted, disgraced, despised, attacked, and profaned. The holy angels, more powerful than all the armies of the world, are restrained and not allowed to strike evil men down for their blasphemies against the Holy Eucharist. What holds them back? God's love and goodness hold them back. The goodness of God is so great that the Heavenly Father allows his Son to be mocked in the Holy Eucharist in order to conquer hearts through sacrificial, self-emptying love. As our Retreat Master notes, Jesus is now insulted even more than when he was hanging from the Cross at Calvary. Our beloved Jesus is so in love with us that he is willing to undergo endless insults in order to win our hearts and bring us to his kingdom.

Why does God allow himself to be treated with such derision, contempt, and betrayal? Why not strike down such evildoers? God's goodness seems scandalous, reckless, and without reason. If you were God, you would most likely punish those who attacked you and spit on you. But God's ways are not our ways. God's goodness is not overcome by sinners. God's love is not conquered by hate. On the contrary, Jesus conquers evil and hate with love, real sacrificial love. This love and goodness is perfectly manifested in the Holy Eucharist where Jesus leaves himself exposed to the insults and blasphemies of all mankind. He is truly in love with fallen humanity. He is in love with you.

Nonetheless, God's goodness should not be taken advantage of or abused. In our times, some in leadership positions warn people not to "weaponize the Eucharist," and offer very confusing messages by seemingly encouraging everyone to receive Holy Communion, regardless of the state of their soul. For example, people living in unnatural relationships, those committing intrinsically disordered actions, and those who are in adulterous relationships are encouraged to receive

Holy Communion. This is wrong. Such thinking is very dangerous and destructive to souls and their ultimate well-being. We must never forget what St. Paul told the early Christians in Corinth about sacrilegious reception of the Holy Eucharist (see 1 Corinthians 11:26–30). Our Retreat Master makes a very strong point on this matter: "Sinners who receive him unworthily crucify him in their soul and unite themselves to a demon, who are their own sovereign master!"[2]

Without a doubt, the Eucharist is not a prize for the perfect. Every devout Catholic understands that. Every pious follower of Jesus also knows that the Eucharist is nourishment for the weak and a powerful medicine for the soul, but they also know that Holy Communion is not food to be given to those in mortal sin. Unworthy reception of Holy Communion does no good to a person who receives it in a state of mortal sin. In fact, it does the opposite. Unworthy reception of the Eucharist greatly harms a soul and their relationship with God and the Church. Unworthy reception of Holy Communion does not heal a person, but, rather, compounds sin, leading to confusion and scandal. That is not what God wants, and people should not take advantage of God's goodness in such a manner.

God's goodness is meant to be respected and treasured, not abused and insulted. This is why God's goodness provides us with the ability to go to Confession. Repentance through the Sacrament of Reconciliation (Confession) is the medicine applied first for the soul in mortal sin, not Holy Communion. God's goodness in the Eucharist wants to be consumed, but in the proper order and manner. Good medicine applied to the wrong wound does no good. Confession reconciles those in mortal sin to God and puts them back in a state of grace so that they can partake of the goodness of God in the Eucharist. It doesn't work the other way around.

Give thanks to Jesus for his goodness in the Eucharist. Praise him for his love, mercy, and desire to be received by you in Holy Communion. His goodness is for you. Always seek to reciprocate that goodness by doing all you can to receive him worthily and free of mortal sin. Then, your union with the Eucharist will be transformative, life-giving, and a blessing.

Reflection Questions

1. Why does our Eucharistic Lord permit himself to be treated so poorly?
2. How is the Holy Eucharist a sign of God's goodness?
3. Why should people not abuse God's goodness by receiving Holy Communion in mortal sin?

Resolution

Today, implore our Eucharistic Lord to give you the grace to respond to his goodness by resolving never to receive him in a state of mortal sin. Say a prayer of reparation to the Eucharistic heart of Jesus for those who receive him unworthily and abuse his goodness.

Prayer

Dear Jesus, my Eucharistic Lord, your goodness is insulted daily by those who receive you in a state of mortal sin. I praise you for your love and mercy that do not strike the sinner for the many sacrileges committed. Forgive us and conquer our hearts with your mercy and goodness. Our Lady of the Most Blessed Sacrament, keep me from all sin and help me to surrender to God's goodness. Saint Joseph, help me to make reparation to the Eucharistic heart of Jesus. Saint Peter Julian Eymard, Apostle of the Eucharist, fill me with your Eucharistic zeal so that I might love the Blessed Sacrament above all things.

Pray the Litany of the Most Precious Blood (page 166)

DAY 27
The Most Solemn Moment

Retreat Master: St. Peter Julian Eymard

The most solemn moments of your life are those you spend in thanksgiving, when the King of heaven and earth, your Savior and your judge, is yours, fully inclined to grant all you ask of him. Rather than abridge your thanksgiving, it would be better, if necessary, to shorten your preparation instead; for there is no more holy, no more salutary moment for you than when you possess Jesus in your body and in your soul.[1]

The temptation often comes to shorten our thanksgiving. The devil knows its value; and our nature, our self-love, shrinks from its effects. Determine, therefore, what the duration of your thanksgiving is to be and subtract never a moment from it without a pressing reason. Thanksgiving is absolutely necessary if the act of Communion, so holy, is not to degenerate into a mere pious habit.[2]

Reflection

There is no more holy moment than when you possess Jesus in your body and soul.

The temptation often comes to shorten our thanksgiving.

Thanksgiving is absolutely necessary.

Our Retreat Master is not alone in stating that the time spent in thanksgiving after receiving Holy Communion is the most solemn moment of your life. Many saints echo this same thought. Saint John Baptist de La Salle states, "Be convinced that there is in all your life no more precious time than that of Holy Communion and the moments immediately following, during which you have the happiness to be able to speak face-to-face, heart-to-heart, with Jesus."[3] Mental prayer, spiritual reading, praying the Rosary, and reading the Bible are all very important things for your spiritual life, but nothing compares to the reception of Holy Communion and the spiritual intimacy afterward.

> The minutes that follow Communion are the most precious we have in our lives. They are the minutes best suited on our part for being with God, and on his part for communicating his love to us.[4]
> — St. Mary Magdalene de' Pazzi

Preparation for Holy Mass is very important too. Arriving early to Mass so that you can pray and prepare your heart is a wonderful habit to acquire. Meditating on the readings the night before or praying a rosary on the way to church are also ways you can prepare your heart for Holy Mass. Doing some form of preparation is very important. Yet, as good as preparation is, it is the time of thanksgiving after Holy Communion that should never be neglected. Jesus is in your heart. It is the most solemn moment of your life.

The devil knows this and doesn't want you to give thanks. He knows there is power and incredible graces given to those who spend time after Mass giving thanks for the gift of the Eucharist. The devil would much prefer you to treat the Eucharist as a dead object, getting out of church as soon as possible, and moving on to the next thing in life. In your average parish, how many people rush out of church immediately after Mass? Almost everyone. It is rare to see people stay, kneel in prayer, and give thanks for even a few minutes. Most parishes become a flurry of activity after Mass. Even the pastor leaves and goes outside to shake everyone's hand. It's a nice gesture, of course, but how many people have ever seen their priest kneel down and give thanks for the Eucharist after Mass? Not many. If a father (spiritual or biological) does not give their children an example of Eucharistic thanksgiving, how will the children (parishioners or family members) learn that the reception of Holy Communion is the most solemn moment of their lives?

Ponder the story of the one leper who returned to thank Jesus for healing him.

> As he continued his journey to Jerusalem, he traveled through Samaria and Galilee. As he was entering a village, ten lepers met him. They stood at a distance from him and raised their voice, saying, "Jesus, Master! Have pity on us!" And when he saw them, he said, "Go show yourselves to the priests." As they were going they were cleansed. And one of them, realizing he had been healed, returned, glorifying God in a loud voice; and he fell at the feet of Jesus and thanked him. He was a Samaritan. Jesus said in reply, "Ten were cleansed, were they not? Where are the other nine? Has none but this foreigner returned to give thanks to God?" Then he said to him, "Stand up and go; your faith has saved you." (Luke 17:11–19)

Do you give thanks for the blessing of receiving the Eucharist? It is the most solemn moment of your life.

Reflection Questions

1. What are the most solemn moments of your life, and where does Holy Communion rank among those moments?
2. How does the devil seek to diminish your Eucharistic thanksgiving?
3. How can you do a better job of preparing and giving thanks for Mass and Holy Communion?

Resolution

Today, resolve to spend at least five minutes in thanksgiving the next time you attend Holy Mass. It may be difficult to pray because of all the distractions and noise, but let the world pass you by. Tell Jesus you are truly grateful for Holy Communion.

Prayer

Dear Jesus, my Eucharistic Lord, I praise you for coming to me in Holy Communion. I am like the leper healed of sin, and yet I have so often not returned to give you thanks. Help me to make this correction in my spiritual life. Our Lady of the Most Blessed Sacrament, whose entire life was one of thanksgiving, help me to be grateful for every Holy Communion. Saint Joseph, teach me to never take Holy Communion for granted. Saint Peter Julian Eymard, Apostle of the Eucharist, fill me with your Eucharistic zeal so that I might love the Blessed Sacrament above all things.

Pray the Litany of the Holy Eucharist (page 163)

DAY 28
Eucharistic Thanksgiving

Retreat Master: St. Peter Julian Eymard

Having received Jesus and enthroned him in your heart, remain quiet for a moment, not praying in words, but resting in silent adoration; like Zacchaeus, like Magdalen, prostrate yourself in spirit with the Most Holy Virgin at the feet of Jesus; contemplate him, filled with wonder at the sight of his love. Proclaim him the King of your heart, spouse of your soul, and hearken to his voice. Say to him: "Speak, Lord, for your servant hears." Lay your heart at the feet of the heavenly King. Offer your will to execute his commands; consecrate all your senses to his divine service. Bind your intelligence to his throne that it may never more go astray.

Do not disturb your soul so long as it is recollected, at peace in the presence of the Lord; in this gentle slumber on the heart of Jesus, it receives grace which nourishes it, unites it most sweetly to its beloved, and profits it more than any other spiritual exercise.[1]

The best model for our thanksgiving is Mary receiving the Word in her womb. The most pleasing reception we can make Jesus, and the one best and most rich in graces for us, is to join with his Blessed Mother in adoring him present in our hearts.[2]

Reflection

Remain quiet for a moment, not praying in words, but resting in silent adoration.

The best model for our thanksgiving is Mary.

Join with his Blessed Mother in adoring him.

The Virgin Mary received Jesus perfectly. This was true at the Annunciation and Bethlehem, as well as every occasion she received her divine Son in Holy Communion. She knows best how to teach us and conform us to her son. Jesus wants to give us immeasurable graces in Holy Communion, and having Mary with us will ensure that not one of them is lost. For this reason, it is a very good practice to invoke her before, during, and after we receive Holy Communion. Mary wants all of her spiritual children to make a proper thanksgiving after Holy Communion.

> If you wish to assist at Mass profitably and to secure its many precious fruits, unite yourself as intimately as possible with the Blessed Virgin.[3]
> — Blessed William Joseph Chaminade

> Devotion to our Lord Jesus Christ and devotion to Mary are intimately united. The more we love Jesus Christ in the Blessed Sacrament, the more we love the Blessed Virgin; and the more we love the Blessed Virgin, the more we love the Blessed Sacrament.[4]
> — St. Mary Euphrasia Pelletier

The saints are experts in knowing Our Lady and imitating her Eucharistic thanksgiving. They united their hearts with her Immaculate Heart and reaped abundant fruit from always going to Jesus through Mary. The saints know that there has never been another human person as close to Jesus as Mary. The Virgin Mary knows Jesus better than anyone.

Mary wants all her spiritual children to benefit fully from their reception of Holy Communion. A mother always wants what is best for her children. When you unite your Eucharistic thanksgiving with Mary's, the Holy Trinity sees Mary in you and pours out tremendous blessings. Where Mary is present, the Holy Spirit is present in a particularly fruitful way, and dispensing extraordinary graces. Graces of conversion, healing, peace, joy, love, and trust.

The cave in Bethlehem, where Mary laid the Child
Jesus, was the first of all tabernacles, and the poor
clothes that wrapped him were the first corporals.
How could I approach the Eucharist, how could
I receive it in my heart without thinking about
Mary? To whom is it that I owe that treasure of my
soul, that divine life, the seed of purity from my
heart, if not through the Eucharist given through
Mary?[5]

— Blessed Concepción Cabrera de Armida

As Our Lady knelt before the crib in Bethlehem and
adored her divine child, and as she bowed her head in silent
adoration and prayer after receiving Holy Communion, your
thanksgiving after Holy Communion should be a time of
awe and wonder as well. The time you spend in thanksgiving
doesn't have to be filled with words or poetic prayers. Silent
contemplation of God inside you is the Marian way to give
thanks for the gift of the Eucharist. Words may come, intentions may flow, but there is no need to force it. Adore him. Be
still and know that he is God. Be like Mary.

Reflection Questions

1. Why is being united with Our Lady the best way
   to give thanks after Holy Communion?
2. How can Mary's example help you to make a
   better Eucharistic thanksgiving?
3. Can you spend a few minutes in silent adoration
   after receiving Holy Communion?

Resolution

Today, ask Our Lady to help you be more like her in your
Eucharistic thanksgiving. Invite her to always be with you
after Holy Communion so that you can adore Jesus and give
him thanks.

Prayer

Dear Jesus, my Eucharistic Lord, I adore your Real Presence in the Blessed Sacrament. Make me more like the Virgin Mary. I want to be receptive, grateful, prayerful, and fruitful in the spiritual life. Our Lady of the Most Blessed Sacrament, be a mother to me and teach me how to be united with Jesus in Holy Communion. Saint Joseph, give me a greater love for Jesus and Mary. Saint Peter Julian Eymard, Apostle of the Eucharist, fill me with your Eucharistic zeal so that I might love the Blessed Sacrament above all things.

Pray the Litany of the Most Precious Blood (page 166)

DAY 29
Eucharistic Union

Retreat Master: St. Peter Julian Eymard

Jesus Christ desires an intimate union with every soul. That is why he instituted the Holy Eucharist, wherein are celebrated each day his nuptials with the Christian soul. And it is our souls that are invited, not only to be present at the feast but to become the spouses of Jesus Christ.[1]

It is true that Jesus Christ, for his part, could in one Communion make us perfect and entirely united with him. That is what he desires to do. But we are so far from being rid of the dross of our nature, so unfit to become part of him that Jesus has to renew the union frequently in order to strengthen and perfect our first Communion. Each time he confirms the first union and makes it purer and closer. Jesus does not give himself partially, and the imperfection of the union is not his doing, but ours; we are not ready for it and we hesitate to lose ourselves in him.[2]

Let us, then, honor Jesus as our divine Spouse. Let us love him with all the devotion of which we are capable. Ah, but we, unfaithful, have sinned and failed to keep our promises! Jesus has loved us in spite of our faults and he invites us now to renew our union with him. He forgets all our offenses, and shall we not love him? Shall we not promise him from the depths of our hearts an inviolable fidelity?[3]

Until we have a passionate love for our Lord in the Most Blessed Sacrament, we shall accomplish nothing. Certainly, our Lord loves us passionately in the Eucharist; he loves us blindly without a thought for himself, devoting himself entirely for our good. We should love him as he loves us.[4]

Reflection

Jesus Christ desires an intimate union with every soul.

Let us love him with all the devotion of which we are capable.

We should love him as he loves us.

In Sacred Scripture, God uses the imagery of spousal love to communicate how much he loves us and wants us to be with him. Christ is the bridegroom; the Church is his bride. This means that every soul in the Church is united with him in a bond of covenant love. You might be inclined to think that only religious sisters are united with God in spiritual marriage. But this is not the case. Every baptized person is spiritually espoused to God and called to the heavenly wedding feast of the Lamb. Our Lord is not content with being our Savior, friend, and brother. He wants to be our all! This is why he instituted the Eucharist.

> The greatest love story of all time is contained in a tiny white host.[5]
>
> — Venerable Fulton J. Sheen

On the eve of his Passion and death, Jesus gave his bride, the Church, the Holy Eucharist. It is his greatest treasure. It is he himself truly present, a love that longs to be consumed. As married couples generally give each other a gift (a present) on their wedding anniversary every year, our Eucharistic Lord gives a gift (his presence) every day. This gift surpasses all other gifts. It is not offered once a year, but daily! Our Lord gives himself to us in the Eucharist so that we never forget him and fall more in love with him day after day. He is the Way, the Truth, and the Life. Outside of him, we cannot have eternal life. Only God's love could think of something so sublime and yet so simple as the Holy Eucharist. Jesus is madly in love with us. Jesus is madly in love with you.

How can you be certain that Jesus loves you? How can you reciprocate love from a finite creature to an eternal God?

For man it is impossible, but all things are possible with God. He knows we are incapable of such things, but he has made a way for us. The Eucharist is God's way of giving us absolute certainty that he loves us, and by our worthy reception of Holy Communion, that we are able to give God all that he wants and deserves. He wants our whole being, heart, mind, body, and soul. Our Retreat Master states, "True love looks not at what it gives but at what its beloved deserves."[6] Jesus, our beloved, deserves nothing less than our everything. If we truly love Jesus we do not count the cost it takes for us to give ourselves entirely to him, but empty ourselves of sin and allow ourselves to be united with him through the Eucharist in pure spiritual love. As creatures, we do not have the ability to bring about such a divine union. But God gives us the means to make it happen. The means is the Most Holy Eucharist.

Do you want to be united with God in a profound and intense love, a love so personal and intense that no other love compares? Wouldn't you pay anything and give away all you owned to obtain it? Well, the great news (the Gospel) is that you have access to such union with God on a daily basis. It's free. The Eucharist is everything!

> If souls understood what treasure they possess in the divine Eucharist, it would be necessary to protect tabernacles with impregnable ramparts; because in the delirium of a holy and devouring hunger, they would go themselves to feed on the Manna of the Seraphim. Churches, at night as in daytime, would overflow with worshipers wasting away with love for the august prisoner.[7]
>
> — Blessed Dina Bélanger

I urge you with all the strength of my soul to approach the Eucharistic Table as often as possible. Feed on this Bread of Angels from which you will draw the strength to fight inner struggles, the struggles against passions and against all adversities, because Jesus Christ has promised to those who feed themselves with the Most Holy Eucharist, eternal life and the necessary graces to obtain it.[8]

— Blessed Pier Giorgio Frassati

Reflection Questions

1. Our Eucharistic Lord desires the greatest intimacy with you. Do you put up any barriers to such intimacy?
2. Jesus is the lover of your soul. How does this reality impact your relationship with him?
3. What are some practical ways you can try to love our Eucharistic Lord as he loves you?

Resolution

Today, ask our Eucharistic Lord for the grace to have the greatest union possible with him in the Blessed Sacrament. Express your desire to always live in union with him and never do anything that offends him.

Prayer

Dear Jesus, my Eucharistic Lord, help me to love you without reserve, holding nothing back. Thank you for the availability of receiving you in Holy Communion every day. Our Lady of the Most Blessed Sacrament, give me a share in your love for Jesus in Holy Communion. Saint Joseph, never let me separate myself from Jesus in the Holy Eucharist. Saint Peter Julian Eymard, Apostle of the Eucharist, fill me with your Eucharistic zeal so that I might love the Blessed Sacrament above all things.

Pray the Litany of the Holy Eucharist (page 163)

DAY 30
The Holy Eucharist and Death

Retreat Master: St. Peter Julian Eymard

Why has our Lord willed to establish so close a relation between the Sacrament of the Eucharist and his death? It was, in the first place, to remind us of the price this Sacrament cost him. The Eucharist, in fact, is the fruit of the death of Jesus.[1]

Jesus gave me the greatest proof of his love when he went to his death in order to make the Eucharist possible and give it to me. How many think of this price paid for by the Eucharist? And yet Jesus is there to remind us of it. But like ungrateful children we are bent only on using and enjoying our riches without ever thinking of the one who acquired them for us at the cost of his life.[2]

Another reason for our Lord's linking the idea of death to the Eucharist is to tell us over and over again what ought to be in us concerning the effects of the Eucharist. The first effect is to make us die to sin and our vicious inclinations. The second is to make us die to the world and to crucify us with Jesus Christ. The third is to make us die to ourselves, to our preferences, to our desires, to our senses so that we may put on Jesus Christ; in other words, that Jesus Christ may live in us, and that we may be his members, docile to his will. The last is to make us share in his glorious Resurrection.[3]

Communion prepares us for heaven. What a great grace to die after having received Holy Viaticum! I know that perfect contrition justifies us and gives us a right to heaven; but how much better to go in company with Jesus, and to be judged by his love, still united, so to speak, with his Sacrament of Love! It is for this reason that the Church wishes her priests to administer Holy Viaticum even at the last moment to the well-disposed penitent.

Let us often beg the grace of receiving Holy Viaticum before dying. It will be the pledge of our eternal happiness.[4]

Reflection

The Eucharist is the fruit of the death of Jesus.

Communion prepares us for heaven.

Let us beg the grace of receiving Holy Viaticum before dying.

Instituting the Holy Eucharist cost Jesus everything. His precious blood was poured out on the Cross so that souls could receive Holy Communion. Like seed scattered on the ground, producing fruit, Jesus' blood was sprinkled on Mount Calvary to produce the greatest food known to mankind, the Holy Eucharist. Pious tradition tells us that Golgotha (the place of the skull) is where Adam, the first man, was buried. Jesus, the New Adam, desiring to regenerate humanity, was crucified above Adam's skull, watering the ground with his blood, so that from the new tree of life a food could be given to fallen humanity that gives eternal life to all who eat it.

We often forget just how much suffering went into the institution of the Holy Eucharist. God had the Eucharist in mind from the beginning of creation. It was not an afterthought. When the Second Person of the Holy Trinity took on human nature to save us, the institution of the Eucharist consumed the heart of Jesus. From childhood to manhood, the institution of the Eucharist was his greatest desire.

Jesus is the only person in history who knew how and when he was going to die. He knew it before he was born. He knew these things because he is God. If, in his divine mind, he could have thought of a better method than the Holy Eucharist to save us, he would have done it. There is nothing better than the Eucharist! There is no greater gift he could have given us than himself.

Jesus loves you so much that he wants to remain with you all the days of your life. He is consumed with thinking of you. He wants you to desire him too. He doesn't want you to forget him. Every time you gaze upon the Sacred Host, our Lord wants you to know how much he loved you and was thinking of you 2,000 years ago in Bethlehem, Egypt, Nazareth, and Jerusalem, and how much he loves you and thinks of you now. At every Holy Mass and in every consecrated host in a tabernacle, you continue to be on his mind. Is he on yours?

The Mass is preparation for heaven, and the Holy Eucharist will get you there. Pray for the grace to receive Viaticum before you die. Viaticum literally means "with you on the way" and is when Holy Communion is given to a soul one last time before they die. Ask Our Lady and St. Joseph to obtain this special grace for you. What better way to die than to pass from this life having received Holy Communion one last time.

As a fruit of this retreat, hopefully you have grown in your desire to live a Eucharistic-centered life, no longer taking the Eucharist for granted but experiencing a Eucharistic revival in your soul. Be pious, reverent, and pray about many of the things you learned in this book, even the things that challenged you. The Eucharist is your greatest treasure. Do not let life pass you by without maintain a loving relationship with Jesus in the Blessed Sacrament and always giving thanks for the gift of Holy Communion. Jesus loves you with an eternal love. Love him back. Receive him worthily, go to Confession frequently, genuflect well, visit him often, and speak of his Real Presence to others. Then, when your last breath comes, you will know that Jesus is waiting for you on the other side of the veil.

The Eucharist is my highway to heaven.[5]

— Blessed Carlo Acutis

Reflection Questions

1. How can you be more grateful for the suffering Jesus endured to give you the Holy Eucharist?
2. What are the effects of Holy Communion in your soul, and how can you better respond to these graces?
3. Have you asked the Lord for the gift of dying in his grace and receiving Holy Viaticum?

Resolution

Today, unite yourself more fully to Jesus in the Blessed Sacrament. Give him your past, present, and future. Beg him for the grace to receive Holy Viaticum before you die.

Prayer

Dear Jesus, my Eucharistic Lord, thank you for this retreat. I believe in your Real Presence and never want to be separated from you. Continue to revive my soul through Confession and Holy Communion. Keep me from sin, watch over me always, and root out from my life anything that is not pleasing to you. I'm sorry for all the times I offended your Eucharistic heart and for any time I have taken the Eucharist for granted. Fill me with your Holy Spirit that I might visit you in the tabernacle often, adore you from my every location, and die having received you in Holy Viaticum. I love you, Jesus! I love you in the Most Blessed Sacrament! Our Lady of the Most Blessed Sacrament, help me to be like you and live for the Eucharist. Saint Joseph, Patron of a Happy and Holy Death, may I experience a death like yours, embraced by Jesus and Mary. Saint Peter Julian Eymard, Apostle of the Eucharist, fill me with your Eucharistic zeal so that I might love the Blessed Sacrament above all things.

Pray the Litany of the Most Precious Blood (page 166)

PRAYERS

Litany of the Holy Eucharist

Lord, have mercy.   *Lord, have mercy.*

Christ, have mercy.   *Christ, have mercy.*

Lord, have mercy.   *Lord, have mercy.*

Christ, hear us.   *Christ, graciously hear us.*

God, the Father of Heaven,   *have mercy on us.*

God, the Son, the Redeemer of the world, *have mercy on us.*

God the Holy Spirit,   *have mercy on us.*

Holy Trinity, One God,   *have mercy on us.*

Living Bread, Descended from Heaven,   *have mercy on us.*

Hidden God and Savior,   *have mercy on us.*

Grain of the Chosen,   *have mercy on us.*

Vine Bringing Forth Virgins,   *have mercy on us.*

Bread of Plenty and Delight of Kings,   *have mercy on us.*

Yoke of Sacrifice,   *have mercy on us.*

Pure Offering,   *have mercy on us.*

Lamb without Blemish,   *have mercy on us.*

Table of Offering,   *have mercy on us.*

Food of Angels,   *have mercy on us.*

Hidden Manna,   *have mercy on us.*

Memorial of the Marvels of God,   *have mercy on us.*

Supersubstantial Bread,   *have mercy on us.*

Word made Flesh, Dwelling among us,   *have mercy on us.*

Holy Sacrifice,   *have mercy on us.*

Cup of Blessing,   *have mercy on us.*

Mystery of Faith,   *have mercy on us.*

Most Excellent and Venerable Sacrament, *have mercy on us.*

Sacrifice Most Holy of All,   *have mercy on us.*

True Propitiation for the Living and the Dead,

                             have mercy on us.

Heavenly Antidote, Preserving us from Sin,

                             have mercy on us.

Most Holy Commemoration of the Passion of the Lord,
have mercy on us.
Gift Transcending all Plenitude, *have mercy on us.*
Memorial Worthy of Divine Love, *have mercy on us.*
Outpouring of Divine Generosity, *have mercy on us.*
Mystery Most Holy and August, *have mercy on us.*
Medicine of Immortality, *have mercy on us.*
Tremendous and Life-Giving Sacrament, *have mercy on us.*
Omnipotent Bread of the Word made Flesh,
have mercy on us.
Unbloody Sacrifice, *have mercy on us.*
Banquet and Guest, *have mercy on us.*
Sweetest Banquet, where Angels Stand as Servants,
have mercy on us.
Sacrament of Piety, *have mercy on us.*
Chain of Charity, *have mercy on us.*
Gift and Giver, *have mercy on us.*
Spiritual Sweetness, Tasted from the Font, *have mercy on us.*
Refreshment of Holy Souls, *have mercy on us.*
Viaticum of those Dying in the Lord, *have mercy on us.*
Pledge of Future Glory, *have mercy on us.*

Be merciful. *Spare us, O, Lord.*
Be merciful. *Graciously hear us, O Lord.*

From unworthy reception of your Body, *save us, O Lord.*
From the lusts of the flesh, *save us, O Lord.*
From the lusts of the eyes, *save us, O Lord.*
From pride of life, *save us, O Lord.*
From every occasion of sin, *save us, O Lord.*

Through your desire to eat the Passover with your disciples,
save us, O Lord.
Through that highest humility, by which you washed the
feet of your disciples, *save us, O Lord.*

Through that most ardent charity, with which you instituted
this Sacrament,   *save us, O Lord.*

Through your Precious Blood, which you left us on the altar,
save us, O Lord.

Through the five wounds on your Most Holy Body,
save us, O Lord.

We sinners beseech you,   *hear us.*

Deign to increase and preserve us in faith and devotion to
this Sacrament,   *we beseech you, hear us.*

Deign to lead us to frequent reception of the Eucharist,
through true confession of sins,   *we beseech you, hear us.*

Deign to liberate us from all heresy and blindness of heart,
we beseech you, hear us.

Deign to obtain for us the precious and heavenly fruit of
this holy Sacrament,   *we beseech you, hear us.*

Deign to comfort and strengthen us in the hour of our death,
we beseech you, hear us.

Lamb of God, who takes away the sins of the world,
spare us, O Lord.

Lamb of God, who takes away the sins of the world,
graciously hear us, O Lord.

Lamb of God, who takes away the sins of the world,
have mercy on us.

You have given them bread from heaven.
Man has eaten the bread of angels.

Let us pray: O God, who in this miraculous Sacrament have
left us a memorial of your Passion; grant, we beseech you,
that we may revere the Sacred Mysteries of your Body and
Blood, and may experience the fruit of redemption within
us, who lives and reigns with the Father in the unity of the
Holy Spirit, God forever and ever. Amen.[1]

Litany of the Most Precious Blood

Lord, have mercy.   *Lord, have mercy.*
Christ, have mercy.   *Christ, have mercy.*
Lord, have mercy.   *Lord, have mercy.*
Christ, hear us.   *Christ, graciously hear us.*

God, the Father of Heaven,   *have mercy on us.*
God, the Son, the Redeemer of the world, *have mercy on us.*
God, the Holy Spirit,   *have mercy on us.*
Holy Trinity, One God,   *have mercy on us.*

Blood of Christ, only Begotten Son of the Eternal Father,
                                                       save us.
Blood of Christ, of the New and Eternal Testament, *save us.*
Blood of Christ, falling upon the earth in the Agony, *save us.*
Blood of Christ, shed profusely in the Scourging,   *save us.*
Blood of Christ, flowing forth in the Crowning of Thorns,
                                                       save us.
Blood of Christ, poured out on the Cross,   *save us.*
Blood of Christ, price of our salvation,   *save us.*
Blood of Christ, without which there is no forgiveness,
                                                       save us.
Blood of Christ, Eucharistic drink and refreshment of souls,
                                                       save us.
Blood of Christ, stream of mercy,   *save us.*
Blood of Christ, victor over demons,   *save us.*
Blood of Christ, courage of Martyrs,   *save us.*
Blood of Christ, strength of Confessors,   *save us.*
Blood of Christ, bringing forth Virgins,   *save us.*
Blood of Christ, help of those in peril,   *save us.*
Blood of Christ, relief of the burdened,   *save us.*
Blood of Christ, hope of the penitent,   *save us.*
Blood of Christ, consolation of the dying,   *save us.*

Blood of Christ, peace and tenderness of hearts,   *save us.*
Blood of Christ, pledge of eternal life,   *save us.*
Blood of Christ, freeing souls from purgatory,   *save us.*
Blood of Christ, most worthy of all glory and honor, *save us.*

Lamb of God, who takes away the sins of the world,
spare us, O Lord.
Lamb of God, who takes away the sins of the world,
graciously hear us, O Lord.
Lamb of God, who takes away the sins of the world,
have mercy on us.

You have redeemed us, O Lord, in your Blood.
And made us, for our God, a kingdom.

Let us pray: Almighty and eternal God, you have appointed
your only-begotten Son the Redeemer of the world, and
will to be appeased by his Blood. Grant we beg of you,
that we may worthily adore this price of our salvation, and
through its power be safeguarded from the evils of the present life, so that we may rejoice in its fruits forever in heaven.
Through the same Christ our Lord. Amen.

Spiritual Communion Prayer

My Jesus, I believe that you are present in the Most Blessed Sacrament. I love you above all things, and I desire to receive you into my soul. Since I cannot receive you sacramentally, come at least spiritually into my heart. I embrace you as if you were already there, and unite myself wholly to you. Never permit me to be separated from you. Amen.[2]

Prayer to St. Peter Julian Eymard

O Blessed Peter Julian, who received the outstanding privilege of knowing so perfectly the treasures of the Most Holy Eucharist, to be on fire with it with seraphic love and to consecrate your tireless zeal to make it known and glorified perpetually by the whole world, obtain for us, we beg you, the spiritual and temporal graces which we need.

Obtain for us particularly to become, like you, faithful adorers in spirit and in truth of this Great Sacrament, and to work ever more to acquire the Christian virtues, especially a sincere humility, to be able to live a life of union with Jesus Christ which was the constant object of your zeal and which is the principal effect of Holy Communion in our souls.

Finally, obtain for us, O Blessed Peter Julian, your filial devotion to Our Lady of the Blessed Sacrament, in order that we may learn from this dear Mother to serve and adore on earth Jesus veiled in the Eucharist, to be able to adore and glorify him face to face in Heaven. Amen.[3]

About the Author

Father Donald Calloway, MIC, a convert to Catholicism, is a member of the Congregation of the Marian Fathers of the Immaculate Conception. Before his conversion to Catholicism, he was a high school dropout who had been kicked out of a foreign country, institutionalized twice, and thrown in jail multiple times. After his radical conversion, he earned a B.A. in Philosophy and Theology from the Franciscan University of Steubenville, Ohio; M.Div. and S.T.B. degrees from the Dominican House of Studies in Washington, D.C.; and an S.T.L. in Mariology from the International Marian Research Institute in Dayton, Ohio.

In addition to *Under the Mantle: Marian Thoughts from a 21st Century Priest* (Marian Press, 2013), he has written *No Turning Back: A Witness to Mercy* (Marian Press, 2010), a bestseller that recounts his conversion story. He also is the author of *Purest of All Lilies: The Virgin Mary in the Spirituality of St. Faustina* (Marian Press, 2008). He introduced and arranged *Marian Gems: Daily Wisdom on Our Lady* (Marian Press, 2014). He is the author of the international bestseller *Consecration to St. Joseph* (Marian Press, 2019), co-author of *Consecration to St. Joseph for Children and Families* (Marian Press, 2022), and author of the graphic novel *The Chaste Heart of St. Joseph* (Marian Press, 2023).

Father Calloway is the Vicar Provincial and Vocation Director for the Mother of Mercy Province.

To learn more about Marian
vocations, visit
Marian.org/vocations
or visit Fr. Calloway's website,
FatherCalloway.com

References

All citations from *Œuvres complètes* are used with permission and graciously provided by Mrs. Valerie Lemariey. Initial quote at the beginning of the book: St. Peter Julian Eymard, *In Light of the Monstrance*, trans. Rev. Charles De Keyser (New York: Sentinel Press, 1947), 212.

INTRODUCTION

1 Pierre-Julien Eymard, *Œuvres complètes*, 17 vols., Centro Eucaristico (Ponteranica) — Nouvelle Cité (Bruyères-le-Châtel) 2008. Tholin-Bost (Mme.), October 22, 1851 (CO 286; II, 328).

2 The 17-volume critical edition of the works of St. Peter Julian Eymard in French can be viewed at this website: http://www.eymard.org.

3 With the generous help of the Congregation of the Blessed Sacrament, Marian Press obtained several quotes from the unfinished English translation of St. Peter Julian Eymard's collected works. However, since the critical English edition is not finished, the vast majority of quotes from St. Peter Julian Eymard in *30 Day Eucharistic Revival* are taken from previous English translations of the saint's works that were published in the 19th and 20th centuries. Since the previous English translations were done with the approval of the Congregation of the Blessed Sacrament, it is understood that the forthcoming critical English edition might have differences in wording and style than the previous English translations, but the essence of St. Peter Julian Eymard's thought remains the same.

4 Pierre-Julien Eymard, *Œuvres complètes*, February 11, 1852 (CO 325; II, 378).

MEET THE RETREAT MASTER: ST. PETER JULIAN EYMARD

1 St. Peter Julian Eymard, as quoted in Ann Ball, *Modern Saints: Their Lives and Faces, Book One* (Charlotte, NC: TAN Books, 2011), 60.

2 St. Peter Julian Eymard, *Life and Letters of Saint Peter Julian Eymard: Volume 3 (1858–1861)*, trans. Sr. Catherine Marie Caron, SSS (Rome: Curia Generalizia Congregation of the Blessed Sacrament, 2010), 11.

RETREAT PREPARATION

[1] Pierre-Julien Eymard, *Œuvres complètes*, The Month of the Most Blessed Sacrament, June 1, 1865 (PP 14, 2; XII, 659).

[2] St. Peter Julian Eymard, Eucharistic Handbook (New York: Sentinel Press, 1958), 262–263.

DAY 1: GOD'S ETERNAL LOVE

[1] St. Peter Julian Eymard, *The Eucharist and Christian Perfection* (Part I), trans. Amy Allen (New York: Sentinel Press, 1948), 164.

DAY 2: GOD'S PERSONAL LOVE

[1] St. Peter Julian Eymard, *Holy Communion*, trans. Clara Morris Rumball (New York: Sentinel Press, 1940), 153–154.

DAY 3: JESUS'S EUCHARISTIC LOVE

[1] St. Peter Julian Eymard, *Eucharistic Handbook*, 30.

[2] St. Peter Julian Eymard, *The Real Presence: Eucharistic Meditations* (New York: Sentinel Press, 1938), 75.

[3] St. Peter Julian Eymard, *The Real Presence* (New York: Fathers of the Blessed Sacrament, 1907), 83–85.

[4] Ven. Louise Margaret Claret de la Touche, as quoted in *Magnificat* 25, no. 4 (June 2023): 255.

[5] St. Peter Julian Eymard, *The Real Presence*, 75.

[6] Bl. Michael Sopoćko, *God's Amazing Mercy*, ed. Robert Stackpole, STD (Stockbridge, MA: Marian Press, 2022), 125.

[7] St. Peter Julian Eymard, *The Eucharistic and Christian Perfection* (Part I), 167.

DAY 4: LOVE IS NOT LOVED

[1] St. Peter Julian Eymard, *The Real Presence: Eucharistic Meditations*, 148.

[2] Ibid.

[3] Ibid., 150–151.

[4] Ibid., 151.

[5] St. John Eudes, *The Sacred Heart of Jesus* (Fitzwilliam, NH: Loreto Publications, 2011), 89.

[6] St. Faustina Kowalska, *Diary: Divine Mercy in My Soul* (Stockbridge, MA: Marian Press, 2000), 132–133.

[7] St. Manuel González García, as quoted in Keith Jiron, *The*

Mariology of Saint Manuel González García (Madrid: El Granito de Arena, 2022), 37.

DAY 5: SIN

1 St. Peter Julian Eymard, *The Eucharist and Christian Perfection* (New York: Fathers of the Blessed Sacrament, 1912), 7.

2 St. Peter Julian Eymard, *The Eucharist and Christian Perfection* (Part II), trans. Amy Allen (New York: Sentinel Press, 1948), 55.

3 Ibid., 96.

4 Ibid., 97.

5 Ven. Pope Pius XII, "Radio Message of His Holiness Pius XII to Participants in the National Catechetical Congress of the United States in Boston" (October 26, 1946).

6 St. Peter Julian Eymard, *The Eucharist and Christian Perfection* (Part II), 59.

7 St. Claude de la Colombière, *The Spiritual Direction of Saint Claude de la Colombière,* 3rd ed., trans. Mother M. Philip, I.B.V.M. (San Francisco: Ignatius Press, 2018), 29.

8 St. Peter Julian Eymard, *The Eucharist and Christian Perfection* (Part I), 314.

DAY 6: UNWORTHINESS

1 St. Peter Julian Eymard, *Holy Communion*, 2.

2 St. Peter Julian Eymard, *In the Light of the Monstrance*, trans. Rev. Charles De Keyser (New York: Sentinel Press, 1947), 162.

3 Ibid., 162–163.

4 Ibid., 156–157.

5 St. Peter Julian Eymard, *Holy Communion*, 94.

6 Ibid.

7 St. Peter Julian Eymard, *Life and Letters of Saint Peter Julian Eymard: Volume 2 (1853–1857)*, trans. Sr. Catherine Marie Caron, SSS (Rome: Curia Generalizia Congregation of the Blessed Sacrament, 2010), 74.

8 St. Stanislaus Papczyński, *Saint Stanislaus Papczyński Selected Writings*, trans. Casimir Krzyzanowski, MIC, Patrick Lynch, MIC, Thaddaeus Lancton, MIC, and J. R. Thomas Holland (Stockbridge, MA: Marian Heritage, 2022), 659–660.

DAY 7: THE MERCY OF GOD

1 St. Peter Julian Eymard, *The Eucharist and Christian Perfection*, 510.
2 Ibid., 513–515.
3 Ibid., 509.
4 St. Faustina Kowalska, *Diary: Divine Mercy in My Soul*, 1447.

DAY 8: THE DEVIL AND THE HOLY EUCHARIST

1 St. Peter Julian Eymard, *The Real Presence: Eucharistic Meditations*, 154.
2 Ibid., 153.
3 Ibid., 118. Of course, St. Peter Julian Eymard does not mean that we are not to love our neighbors too, as our Lord himself said in the second of his two "Great Commandments" (Mk 22:39). All that we love, however, ultimately must flow from our love of God.
4 St. Peter Julian Eymard, *The Real Presence*, 203.
5 According to the Catholic Church, the Eastern Orthodox churches also retain all seven valid Sacraments, and believe and teach the Real Presence of Jesus in the Eucharist.
6 St. Peter Julian Eymard, *The Real Presence*, 65.
7 St. Peter Julian Eymard, *The Real Presence: Eucharistic Meditations*, 120.
8 St. John Chrysostom, as quoted in St. Alphonsus M. Liguori, *Sermons for All Sundays of the Year* (Dublin: Duffy, 1860), 237.

DAY 9: REPARATION

1 St. Peter Julian Eymard, *In the Light of the Monstrance*, 229.
2 Ibid., 230.
3 St. Peter Julian Eymard, *Life and Letters of Saint Peter Julian Eymard: Volume 1 (1828–1852)*, trans. Sr. Catherine Marie Caron, SSS (Rome: Curia Generalizia Congregation of the Blessed Sacrament, 2010), 196.
4 St. Peter Julian Eymard, *The Real Presence: Eucharistic Meditations*, 12–13.
5 Bl. Basil Moreau, *Basil Moreau: Essential Writings*, ed. Kevin Grove, CSC, and Andrew Gawrych, CSC (Notre Dame, IN: Christian Classics, 2014), 165.
6 Bl. Basil Moreau, *Essential Writings*, 325.

7 Sr. Angela de Fatima Cohelho, *Inside the Light: Understanding the Message of Fatima* (Gastonia, NC: TAN Books, 2020), 58.

DAY 10: PRAYER AND HOLINESS

1 St. Peter Julian Eymard, *Holy Communion*, 235.

2 St. Peter Julian Eymard, *The Real Presence*, 17–18.

3 Pope St. John Paul II, *Mane Nobiscum Domine* (October 7, 2004).

4 Blessed Carlo Acutis, as quoted in Antonia Salzano Acutis, *My Son Carlo: Carlo Acutis through the Eyes of His Mother* (Huntington, IN: Our Sunday Visitor, 2023), 229–230.

5 Ibid, 226.

6 St. Francis De Sales, *Introduction to the Devout Life*. (San Francisco: Ignatius Press, 2015), Chapter 14, 55.

7 Bl. Henry Suso, as quoted in Saint Joseph Adoration Monastery, *Manual for Eucharistic Adoration: The Poor Clares of Perpetual Adoration* (Charlotte, NC: TAN, 2016), 118.

DAY 11: EUCHARISTIC FAITH

1 St. Peter Julian Eymard, *The Real Presence*, 121–123.

2 Ven. Fulton J. Sheen, *The World's First Love: Mary, Mother of God* (San Francisco: Ignatius Press, 1996), 211.

DAY 12: EUCHARISTIC PIETY

1 St. Peter Julian Eymard, *Eucharistic Handbook*, 49.

2 Ibid., 48.

3 Some historians and theologians assert that for the first eight centuries of the Church, Holy Communion was distributed in the hand and not on the tongue. This claim is widely debated. One of the most used statements from the early Church in defense of Holy Communion is attributed to St. Cyril of Jerusalem (4th century):

> In approaching therefore, come not with your wrists extended, or your fingers spread; but make your left hand a throne for the right, as for that which is to receive a King. And having hollowed your palm, receive the Body of Christ, saying over it, *Amen*. So then after having carefully hallowed your eyes by the touch of

the Holy Body, partake of it; giving heed lest you lose any portion thereof; for whatever you lose is evidently a loss to you as it were from one of your own members. For tell me, if anyone gave you grains of gold, would you not hold them with all carefulness, being on your guard against losing any of them, and suffering loss? Will you not then much more carefully keep watch, that not a crumb fall from you of what is more precious than gold and precious stones? Then after you have partaken of the Body of Christ, draw near also to the Cup of his Blood; not stretching forth your hands, but bending, and saying with an air of worship and reverence, "Amen," and hallow yourself by partaking also of the Blood of Christ. And while the moisture is still upon your lips, touch it with your hands, and hallow your eyes and brow and the other organs of sense. Then wait for the prayer, and give thanks unto God, who has accounted you worthy of so great mysteries. Hold fast these traditions undefiled, and keep yourselves free from offense. Sever not yourselves from the Communion; deprive not yourselves, despite the pollution of sins, of these Holy and Spiritual Mysteries. (St. Cyril of Jerusalem, *Catechesis mystagogica* V, xxi–xxii, Migne, *Patrologia Graeca* 33)

Some in the Church dispute the attribution of the above statement to St. Cyril, and for good reason. Was St. Cyril (or an unknown author) writing about Holy Communion being given to the laity in the hand or other priests and deacons? Were people really to wipe their eyes and brows with the Blood of Christ? Isn't that a profanation? Was St. Cyril instructing people to receive Holy Communion regardless of the "pollution of sins"? Attributing this statement to St. Cyril is very suspect. Historically, there is some evidence that if and when the laity received Holy Communion in the hand, a cloth was to be placed over the hands so that no particles fell to the floor. Regardless of these historical issues, it can't be denied that in the eighth century the Latin Rite Church completely abolished the distribution of Holy Communion in the hand. Why did this happen? If it was such a good and noble practice, why did it abruptly end? The reason is that the hierarchy recognized that profanations and abuses were occurring and something had to be done about it. Thus, from the eighth to the 20th centuries, the Latin Rite Church only allowed the lay faithful to receive Holy Communion on the tongue. In modern times, the Church seems to be returning to a contestable ancient practice that, while not sinful in itself, opens the door to various ways of profanation of the Holy Eucharist. This is a serious matter and must be examined and addressed by the hierarchy of the Church.

4   *Redemptionis Sacramentum*, 92.

DAY 13: RECOLLECTION

1   St. Peter Julian Eymard, *In the Light of the Monstrance*, 101.

2   St. Peter Julian Eymard, *Life and Letters of Saint Peter Julian Eymard: Volume 5 (1865–1866)*, trans. Sr. Catherine Marie Caron, SSS (Rome: Curia Generalizia Congregation of the Blessed Sacrament, 2010), 119.

3   Ibid., 95.

4   St. Peter Julian Eymard, *In the Light of the Monstrance*, 102.

5   St. Peter Julian Eymard, *Life and Letters of Saint Peter Julian Eymard: Volume 4 (1862–1864)*, trans. Sr. Catherine Marie Caron, SSS (Rome: Curia Generalizia Congregation of the Blessed Sacrament, 2010), 72.

6   The Catholic Church has many official documents (universal and diocesan) on the proper use of Extraordinary Ministers of Holy Communion. The entire section from *Redemptionis Sacramentum* (March 19, 2004) titled "The Extraordinary Minister of Holy Communion" is provided here:

> [Paragraph 154.] As has already been recalled, "the only minister who can confect the Sacrament of the Eucharist *in persona Christi* is a validly ordained Priest." Hence the name "minister of the Eucharist" belongs properly to the Priest alone. Moreover, also by reason of their sacred Ordination, the ordinary ministers of Holy Communion are the Bishop, the Priest and the Deacon, to whom it belongs therefore to administer Holy Communion to the lay members of

Christ's faithful during the celebration of Mass. In this way their ministerial office in the Church is fully and accurately brought to light, and the sign value of the Sacrament is made complete.

[Paragraph 155.] In addition to the ordinary ministers there is the formally instituted acolyte, who by virtue of his institution is an extraordinary minister of Holy Communion even outside the celebration of Mass. If, moreover, reasons of real necessity prompt it, another lay member of Christ's faithful may also be delegated by the diocesan Bishop, in accordance with the norm of law, for one occasion or for a specified time, and an appropriate formula of blessing may be used for the occasion. This act of appointment, however, does not necessarily take a liturgical form, nor, if it does take a liturgical form, should it resemble sacred Ordination in any way. Finally, in special cases of an unforeseen nature, permission can be given for a single occasion by the Priest who presides at the celebration of the Eucharist.

[Paragraph 156.] This function is to be understood strictly according to the name by which it is known, that is to say, that of extraordinary minister of Holy Communion, and not "special minister of Holy Communion" nor "extraordinary minister of the Eucharist" nor "special minister of the Eucharist," by which names the meaning of this function is unnecessarily and improperly broadened.

[Paragraph 157.] If there is usually present a sufficient number of sacred ministers for the distribution of Holy Communion, extraordinary ministers of Holy Communion may not be appointed. Indeed, in such circumstances, those who may have already been appointed to this ministry should not exercise it. The practice of those Priests is reprobated who, even though present at the celebration, abstain from distributing Communion and hand this function over to laypersons.

[Paragraph 158.] Indeed, the extraordinary minister of Holy Communion may administer Communion only when the Priest and Deacon are lacking, when the Priest is prevented by weakness or advanced age or some other genuine reason, or when the number of faithful coming to Communion is so great that the very celebration of Mass would be unduly prolonged. This, however, is to be understood in such a way that a brief prolongation, considering the circumstances and culture of the place, is not at all a sufficient reason.

[Paragraph 159.] It is never allowed for the extraordinary minister of Holy Communion to delegate anyone else to administer the Eucharist, as for example a parent or spouse or child of the sick person who is the communicant.

[Paragraph 160.] Let the diocesan Bishop give renewed consideration to the practice in recent years regarding this matter, and if circumstances call for it, let him correct it or define it more precisely. Where such extraordinary ministers are appointed in a widespread manner out of true necessity, the diocesan Bishop should issue special norms by which he determines the manner in which this function is to be carried out in accordance with the law, bearing in mind the tradition of the Church.

[7] St. Peter Julian Eymard, *Life and Letters of Saint Peter Julian Eymard: Volume 5*, 162.

DAY 14: REVERENCE AND SILENCE

[1] St. Peter Julian Eymard, *The Real Presence: Eucharistic Meditations*, 163.
[2] St. Peter Julian Eymard, *Eucharistic Handbook*, 101–102.
[3] St. Peter Julian Eymard, *Life and Letters of Saint Peter Julian Eymard: Volume 5*, 103.
[4] Ibid., 128.

DAY 15: EUCHARISTIC ADORATION

[1] St. Peter Julian Eymard, *In the Light of the Monstrance*, 177.
[2] St. Peter Julian Eymard, *The Real Presence*, XI–XII.

³ St. Peter Julian Eymard, *Life and Letters of Saint Peter Julian Eymard: Volume 4*, 311.

⁴ Ordinarily, in daily life, adoration is the most holy action we can perform, but under extraordinary circumstances the highest act of holiness would be to lay down one's life for one's friends, as Jesus said (John 15:13) — one's chief "friend" being God himself, of course (John 15:15).

⁵ Bl. James Alberione, *Mary, Mother and Model: Feasts of Mary* (Boston: Daughters of St. Paul, 1958), 119.

⁶ St. Paul of the Cross, *A Thought for Every Day* (Rome: Passionist General House, 2017), 35.

⁷ Bl. Carlo Acutis, as quoted in Msgr. Anthony Figueiredo, *Blessed Carlo Acutis: 5 Steps to Being a Saint* (London: CTS, 2021), 79–80.

DAY 16: THE SACRED HEART

¹ St. Peter Julian Eymard, *In the Light of the Monstrance*, 224.

² Ibid., 227.

³ St. Peter Julian Eymard, *Life and Letters of Saint Peter Julian Eymard: Volume 5*, 164.

⁴ Ibid., 51.

⁵ Jesus to St. Margaret Mary Alacoque, as quoted in Fr. John Croieset, SJ. *Devotion to the Sacred Heart* (London: Burns & Lambert, 1863), 7–8.

⁶ Bl. Carlo Acutis, in Figueiredo, *Blessed Carlo Acutis*, 79.

⁷ St. Pope John Paul II, *General Audience (June 8, 1994)*, as quoted in Pope John Paul II, *Holy Father, Sacred Heart*, ed. SJ (New York: Herder & Herder, 2004), 187.

⁸ St. Pope John Paul II, *Homily at Mass for the Beatification of Mother Maria Bernardina Jablonska and Mother Maria Karlowska on the Solemnity of the Sacred Heart of Jesus in Zakopane, Poland (June 6, 1997)*, as quoted in Pope John Paul II, *Holy Father, Sacred Heart*, 98.

⁹ St. Paul of the Cross, *A Thought for Every Day*, 36.

¹⁰ Bl. Basil Moreau, *Essential Writings*, 166.

¹¹ Bl. Dina Bélanger, *Autobiography* (Montreal: Les Religieuses de Jesus-Marie, 1997), 138.

¹² St. Faustina Kowalska, *Diary: Divine Mercy in My Soul*, 174.

¹³ St. Joseph Sebastian Pelczar, as quoted in the unpublished

manuscript "Meditation 159: The Piercing of the Heart of Jesus," courtesy of Sr. Mary Joseph Calore, SSCJ.

DAY 17: THE HOLY SPIRIT

[1] St. Peter Julian Eymard, *In the Light of the Monstrance*, 45.

[2] Ibid., 48.

[3] Ibid.

[4] Ibid., 49–50.

[5] St. Peter Julian Eymard, *The Real Presence*, 13.

[6] Bl. Pier Giorgio Frassati, *Letter to Members of "Catholic Youth" of Pollone, Italy* (July 29, 1923).

DAY 18: MARY'S EUCHARISTIC LIFE

[1] St. Peter Julian Eymard. *Eucharistic Handbook*, 124–125.

[2] St. Peter Julian Eymard, *Our Lady of the Most Blessed Sacrament* (New York: Sentinel Press, 1947), 123–124.

[3] Ibid., 132.

[4] Ibid., 132–133.

[5] Ibid., 133.

[6] St. Manuel González García, as quoted in Keith Jiron, *The Mariology of Saint Manuel González García*, 170–171.

[7] Bl. Concepción Cabrera de Armida, as quoted in Kathleen Beckman, *Beautiful Holiness: A Spiritual Journey with Blessed Conchita to the Heart of Jesus* (Manchester, NH: Sophia Institute Press, 2022), 272.

DAY 19: MARY'S INTERIOR LIFE

[1] St. Peter Julian Eymard, *In the Light of the Monstrance*, 231–232.

[2] Ibid., 232.

[3] Ibid., 232–233.

[4] St. Peter Julian Eymard, *Our Lady of the Most Blessed Sacrament*, 132. Prayer is indeed "the great means of salvation," as St. Alphonsus de Liguori titled his famous book, the *sine qua non* of holiness. But without the apostolic succession of bishops, and the Sacrament of Holy Orders, we would not have the greatest form of prayer of all: the Eucharist itself, and the Real Presence of Jesus in the Blessed Sacrament. In that sense, one might say, Holy Orders is equally "the most necessary" of all missions to the Catholic Church.

[5] St. Peter Julian Eymard, *In the Light of the Monstrance*, 233–234.

[6] St. Manuel González García, as quoted in Keith Jiron, *The Mariology of Saint Manuel González García*, 97.

DAY 20: MARY'S SACRIFICIAL LIFE

[1] St. Peter Julian Eymard, *Eucharistic Handbook*, 129–130.

[2] St. Peter Julian Eymard, *Our Lady of the Most Blessed Sacrament*, 124–125.

[3] Jesus to Bl. Concepción Cabrera de Armida, as quoted in Kathleen Beckman, *Beautiful Holiness*, 165.

DAY 21: ST. JOSEPH, THE HUMBLE ADORER

[1] St. Peter Julian Eymard, *Month of St. Joseph*, 23–24.

[2] Ibid., 57–58.

[3] Bl. Basil Moreau, *Essential Writings*, 189.

[4] St. Lawrence of Brindisi, *Opera Omnia: Feastday Sermons*, trans. Vernon Wagner, O.F.M.Cap. (Delhi: Media House, 2007), 539.

[5] Bl. Pope Pius IX, *Quemadmodum Deus* (December 8, 1870).

[6] St. Bernard of Clairvaux, as quoted in St. Peter Julian Eymard, *Month of St. Joseph*, 7.

[7] Ven. Fulton J. Sheen, *The World's First Love: Mary, Mother of God*, 245.

DAY 22: ST. JOSEPH, THE PERPETUAL ADORER

[1] St. Peter Julian Eymard, *Month of St. Joseph*, 32–33.

[2] Bl. Carlo Acutis, in Antonia Salzano Acutis, *My Son Carlo*, 232.

DAY 23: ST. JOSEPH, THE POOR ADORER

[1] St. Peter Julian Eymard, *Month of St. Joseph*, 71–72.

DAY 24: THE HOLY ANGELS

[1] St. Peter Julian Eymard, *The Real Presence*, 256–267.

[2] St. Peter Julian Eymard, *Life and Letters of Saint Peter Julian Eymard: Volume 3 (1858–1861)*, trans. Sr. Catherine Marie Caron, SSS (Rome: Curia Generalizia Congregation of the Blessed Sacrament, 2010), 11.

[3] Ibid., 3.

[4] Ibid., 159.

[5] Ibid., 148.

6 St. Peter Julian Eymard, *Life and Letters of Saint Peter Julian Eymard: Volume 4,* 323.

7 St. Peter Julian Eymard, *Life and Letters of Saint Peter Julian Eymard: Volume 3,* 253.

8 St. Claude De La Colombière, as quoted by Fr. Florian Racine, *Could You Not Watch with Me One Hour?* (San Francisco: Ignatius Press, 2014), 211.

9 St. Peter Julian Eymard, *Life and Letters of Saint Peter Julian Eymard: Volume 4,* 146.

DAY 25: THE CROSS

1 St. Peter Julian Eymard, *Eucharistic Handbook,* 311–312.

2 Ibid., 317–318.

3 Jesus to Bl. Concepción Cabrera de Armida, as quoted in Kathleen Beckman, *Beautiful Holiness,* 183.

DAY 26: GOD'S GOODNESS

1 St. Peter Julian Eymard, *The Real Presence: Eucharistic Meditations,* 129–130.

2 St. Peter Julian Eymard, *The Real Presence,* 83.

DAY 27: THE MOST SOLEMN MOMENT

1 St. Peter Julian Eymard, *Holy Communion,* 51.

2 Ibid., 51.

3 St. John Baptist de La Salle, as quoted in ibid., 51–52.

4 St. Mary Magdalene de' Pazzi, as quoted in Fr. Stefano M. Manelli, FI, *Jesus, Our Eucharistic Love* (New Bedford, MA: Academy of the Immaculate, 2017), 45.

DAY 28: EUCHARISTIC THANKSGIVING

1 St. Peter Julian Eymard, *Holy Communion,* 53.

2 Ibid., 56.

3 Bl. William Joseph Chaminade, *Marian Writings: Volume 2* (Dayton, OH: Marianist Resources Commission, 1980), 280.

4 St. Mary Euphrasia Pelletier, as quoted in *Magnificat* 14, no. 8 (October 2012): 169.

5 Bl. Concepción Cabrera de Armida as quoted in Kathleen Beckman, *Beautiful Holiness,* 185.

DAY 29: EUCHARISTIC UNION

1 St. Peter Julian Eymard, *Holy Communion*, 131.
2 Ibid., 135–136.
3 Ibid.
4 St. Peter Julian Eymard, *The Real Presence: Eucharistic Meditations*, 180.
5 Ven. Fulton J. Sheen, as quoted in Saint Joseph Adoration Monastery, *Manual for Eucharistic Adoration: The Poor Clares of Perpetual Adoration*, 120.
6 St. Peter Julian Eymard, *The Real Presence: Eucharistic Meditations*, 5.
7 Bl. Dina Bélanger, *Autobiography*, 259.
8 Bl. Pier Giorgio Frassati, *Letter to Members of "Catholic Youth" of Pollone, Italy* (July 29, 1923).

DAY 30: THE HOLY EUCHARIST AND DEATH

1 St. Peter Julian Eymard, *The Real Presence: Eucharistic Meditations*, 67.
2 Ibid., 67–68.
3 Ibid., 68.
4 St. Peter Julian Eymard, *The Real Presence*, 362–363.
5 Bl. Carlo Acutis, as quoted in *I Am with You: A Documentary on Carlo Acutis* (Irondale, AL: EWTN, 2021).

PRAYERS

1 *The Litany of the Holy Eucharist* (originally titled *Litany to Christ the Lord on the Holy* Eucharist) was composed by Caspar Keller, SJ, in *Litaniae Catholicae Ad Christum, Beatam Virginem, Et Sanctos* (Ingolstadt: Wilhelm Eder, 1589), 55–61. English translation courtesy of Fr. Robert Nixon, OSB, with slight modifications by Fr. Donald Calloway, MIC.
2 St. Peter Julian Eymard, *Life and Letters of Saint Peter Julian Eymard: Volume 1*, 1.
3 From the *Directory of Prayers of the Servants of the Blessed Sacrament* as quoted in St. Peter Julian Eymard, *Life and Letters of Saint Peter Julian Eymard: Volume 4*, iii.

INSPIRATION FROM FR. CALLOWAY

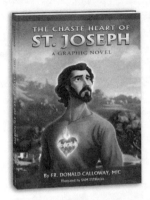 

The Chaste Heart of St. Joseph: A Graphic Novel

Join Fr. Calloway as he tells the dynamic and inspiring story of St. Joseph, our spiritual father and the "Terror of Demons." You'll learn that, whenever you need help, just "Go to Joseph!" Hardcover graphic novel, 84 full-color pages. Y113-JOEG

No Turning Back
A Witness to Mercy, 10th Anniversary Edition

In this 10th anniversary edition, Fr. Calloway looks back on the past decade in a new introduction to this perennially powerful witness to the transforming grace of God and the Blessed Mother's love for her children. His witness proves a key truth of our faith: Between Jesus, the Divine Mercy, and Mary, the Mother of Mercy, there's no reason to give up hope on anyone, no matter how far they are from God. Paperback, 288 pages. Includes photo section. Y113-ANTBK ⓔ

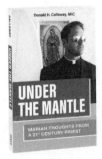

Under the Mantle
Marian Thoughts from a 21st Century Priest

Father Calloway deftly shares his personal insights on topics including the Eucharist, the papacy, the Church, Confession, Divine Mercy, prayer, the Cross, masculinity, and femininity. The Blessed Virgin Mary is the central thread weaving a tapestry throughout with quotes about Our Lady from saints, blesseds, and popes. Paperback. 300 pages. Y113-UTM

Call 1-800-462-7426 or visit FatherCalloway.com

INSPIRATION FROM FR. CALLOWAY

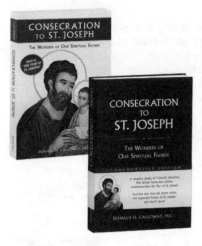

Consecration to St. Joseph: The Wonders of Our Spiritual Father

This book has everything you need to take your love and devotion to St. Joseph to a whole different level: a thorough program of consecration, information on the 10 wonders of St. Joseph, and prayers and devotions to St. Joseph. Y113-FCSJ

Hardcover Commemorative Edition:
Includes a new foreword from Fr. Calloway, 3 ribbons for marking pages, full-color artwork, and lots of other special new material. This will definitely be a keepsake to treasure! Y108-HCJO

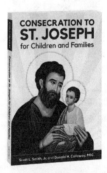

Consecration to St. Joseph for Children and Families

Protect your family! Entrust your family to St. Joseph. Why? Because God Himself did – He entrusted the Holy Family to St. Joseph to keep them safe. Drawing on the wealth of the Church's living tradition, Fr. Donald H. Calloway, MIC and co-author Scott L. Smith, Jr., call on all of us to turn to St. Joseph, entrust ourselves, our children and families, our Church, and our world to our spiritual father's loving care. Watch for wonders when the Universal Patron of the Church opens the floodgates of Heaven to pour out graces into your family's lives. Y113-CJHB

Consecration to St. Joseph for Children and Families Calendar

A colorful calendar and sticker set to go with the book! Kids can chart their progress to Consecration with stickers representing each of the 33 days. Y113-CCSJ

Call 1-800-462-7426 or visit FatherCalloway.com

MARIAN INSPIRATION FROM FR. CALLOWAY

Champions of the Rosary:
The History and Heroes of a Spiritual Weapon

Champions of the Rosary tells the powerful story of the history of the Rosary and the champions of this devotion. The Rosary is a spiritual sword with the power to conquer sin, defeat evil, and bring about peace. Read this book to deepen your understanding and love for praying the Rosary. Endorsed by 30 bishops from around the world! Paperback, 436 pages. Includes photo section. Y113-CRBK 🄴

10 Wonders of the Rosary

The Rosary is presented here in all its wonder: leading armies into battle; defeating the enemies of Christ and His Church; and transforming hearts and minds in order to save societies and entire civilizations. Paperback. 192 pages.
Y113-WOND 🄴

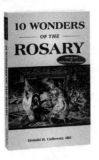

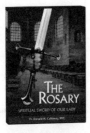

The Rosary
Spiritual Sword of Our Lady DVD

Father Donald Calloway, MIC, explains the power of Our Lady's favorite devotion, the Rosary, in this engaging DVD based on his internationally renowned talks. Y113-RDVD

Eucharistic Gems
Daily Wisdom on The Blessed Sacrament
Y113-EUGM

Rosary Gems
Daily Wisdom on the Holy Rosary
Y113-RGEM

Marian Gems
Daily Wisdom on Our Lady
Y113-MGEM

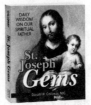

St. Joseph Gems
Daily Wisdom on our Spiritual Father
Y113-SJEM

THE MARIAN FATHERS OF TODAY AND TOMORROW

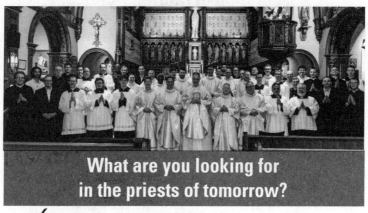

What are you looking for in the priests of tomorrow?

☑ **Zeal for proclaiming the Gospel**
☑ **Faithfulness to Church teaching**
☑ **Love of Mary Immaculate**
☑ **Love of the Holy Eucharist**
☑ **Concern for the souls in Purgatory**
☑ **Dedication to bringing God's mercy to all souls**

These are the top reasons why men pursuing a priestly vocation are attracted to the Congregation of Marian Fathers of the Immaculate Conception.

Please support the education of these future priests.
More than 30 Marian seminarians are counting on your gift.

Call 1-800-462-7426 or visit Marian.org/helpseminarians

YOUR ESSENTIAL DIVINE MERCY RESOURCE

Diary of Saint Maria Faustina Kowalska: Divine Mercy in My Soul

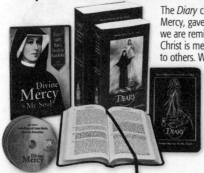

The *Diary* chronicles the message that Jesus, the Divine Mercy, gave to the world through this humble nun. In it, we are reminded to trust in His forgiveness — and as Christ is merciful, so, too, are we instructed to be merciful to others. Written in the 1930s, the *Diary* exemplifies God's love toward mankind and, to this day, remains a source of hope and renewal.

Large Paperback: Y113-NBFD
Compact Paperback: Y113-DNBF
Deluxe Leather-Bound Edition: Y113-DDBURG
Audio *Diary* MP3 Edition: Y113-ADMP3
🄴 Also available as an ebook — Visit shopmercy.org

For our complete line of books, prayer cards, pamphlets, Rosaries, and chaplets, visit ShopMercy.org or call 1-800-462-7426 to have our latest catalog sent to you.

Join the

Association of Marian Helpers,

headquartered at the
National Shrine of The Divine Mercy,
and share in special blessings!

An invitation from
Fr. Joseph, MIC, director

Marian Helpers is an Association of Christian faithful of the Congregation of Marian Fathers of the Immaculate Conception. By becoming a member, you share in the spiritual benefits of the daily Masses, prayers, and good works of the Marian priests and brothers.

This is a special offer of grace given to you by the Church through the Marian Fathers. Please consider this opportunity to share in these blessings, along with others whom you would wish to join into this spiritual communion.

1-800-462-7426 • Marian.org/join

Spiritual Enrollments & Masses

Enroll your loved ones in the Association of Marian Helpers, and they will participate in the graces from the daily Masses, prayers, good works, and merits of the Marian priests and brothers around the world.

Request a Mass to be offered by the Marian Fathers for your loved ones

Individual Masses
(for the living or deceased)

Gregorian Masses
(30 days of consecutive Masses for the deceased)

1-800-462-7426 • Marian.org/enrollments • Marian.org/mass